To Kathleen and Hazel
with best wishes
Susan Stuart

Gladys Maccabe.

Drawing From Memory

The Life of Irish Artist
GLADYS MACCABE
MBE MA(Hons) HRUA HROI FRSA

by

SUSAN STAIRS

with illustrations by
Gladys Maccabe

Shortall-Stairs Publications

Published 2004 by Shortall-Stairs Publications
Dublin 6W, Ireland
Tel: (00 353 1) 4901406 Fax: (00 353 1) 4990507
dshortallart@oceanfree.net
www.myirishart.com

Copyright text © Susan Stairs

All rights reserved. No part of this publication may be reproduced, stored in a retrieval system or transmitted in any form or by any means electronic, mechanical, including photocopying, recording or otherwise, without permission, in writing, from the author, Susan Stairs.

ISBN 0 95347 102 0

Typeset and printed in Ireland by Future Print
Colour photography by Pat Baker
Front cover photography by Derek Shortall
Design by Susan Stairs and Derek Shortall
Binding by Duffy's Bookbinders

FOREWORD

In the last year of the twentieth century, the past occupied our thoughts almost as much as did the future. There was much to look back on. The last one hundred years had seen huge changes – more than had ever taken place in the span of a century - and all around us we could see the evidence of progress and growth. History had been made and, due to the development of film, we could actually see moving pictures of the events that transformed our world. Film is perhaps one of the greatest inventions of them all. For as time advances and the future is drawn towards us, it is possible for us to watch footage of the past; a past which we had hitherto relied on the artist to record. Prior to the advent of photography in the nineteenth century, the artist was entrusted with the very important task of documenting the visual history of our world. It was not until the arrival of the camera that artists began to be less literal, less concerned with the faithful representation of their surroundings. For so long they had striven to depict things as realistically as they could and now, there was a machine which could do that for them. In a way, therefore, it was the camera that set the artist free. Released from the restraints of having to be so precise as to satisfy the demands of the general public, the artist's vision became more personal and he began to paint to satisfy himself.

Much of our memory is shaped by the images we see in books, newspapers and on film. If we read about a historical event that happened many hundreds of years ago, we must rely on our imagination to bring it to life for us. But from now on, our descendants will be able to see exactly how events unfolded. In years to come, they will even be able to see and hear us by playing back videotape recorded today. Imagine how we would be fascinated if we could see film of one of our great-great-great-grandparents; hear them talking; look at how they dressed; see the house they lived in and so on. Our descendants will be able to do this.

Gladys Maccabe has lived her life as an artist during the most exciting century of our world. She has seen more changes than most of us will ever experience; can remember a time when radio was an incredible novelty; when women wore long skirts and dresses and people rarely ventured out without a hat; when the telephone, the motor car and electricity were luxuries afforded only by the few; when an evening spent conversing and playing musical instruments was the most popular form of home entertainment. She has encountered at first hand the terrible events of the Blitz in Belfast and, as a child, experienced the life-changing effects of the Great War.

We know so much about the past century because it has all been recorded for us. We have seen the photographs and watched the film footage. But for all the pictorial evidence at our disposal, it is personal experience which brings it all so very much alive. Individual memory serves to weave the threads of a story together, to suffuse the photographs and drawings with a sensation of understanding. Photographs and paintings of people mean very little to us if their identity is unknown. We can, of course, imagine whatever we wish about them and fancy that we can see in their faces something of their personality – which can indeed be possible. But who is to say how right we are? How much more interesting do they become when we can learn about their life and discover the type of person they really were?

In years to come, it will almost seem as if time travel to the past is possible. There will be so much archival material available that there will be little left about the past to imagine. So much is now documented, in so many formats, that future scholars will have inestimable opportunities to see visual and written evidence about every major event and minor occurrence. There will be no mystery about the past. It will not be the undiscovered region that much of it has been for us.

I believe that everyone has a story to tell about their past. There is not one among us who has nothing interesting to relate. I have chosen to recount the story of Gladys Maccabe because hers is one of triumph and achievement. It is also one of inspiration and faith. We learn from our past and Gladys has much to teach us.

AUTHOR'S NOTE

Fifteen years have passed since I first met Gladys Maccabe and commenced work on the catalogue which accompanied her highly successful retrospective exhibition in 1989. In those years, she has become a special friend to both myself and my family and I have written this book with her full co-operation. Over the past two years or more, she has allowed me access to the personal archive of material that she has gathered over the course of her life. When the idea of a book on her life was first suggested to her, she felt, self-deprecatingly, that she was not worthy of such an honour. Despite her achievements, she has never been one to bask in their glory. Rather, she has spent a large part of her life simply going from one project to the next, without stopping to realise the significance of her accomplishments.

She tells me that some time ago, the Belfast gallery proprietor, Nelson Bell, encouraged her to begin documenting her memories. With so many of her contemporaries having passed on, she was one of a very few still with us who had lived through the years which saw a proliferation of artistic talent in Northern Ireland and she herself had had no small part in its happening. Preferring to speak about, rather than write down, her recollections, she subsequently set about recording a series of audio tapes. These tapes formed the basis for this book. All the major events in her life were recounted, as well as her childhood memories – which go as far back as the day she was born. Stories her own mother told her about her grandparents were also spoken about, reaching back into the latter years of the nineteenth century.

She told of her days in school, her years in college, meeting her husband, Max, and of the birth of her two sons, Christopher and Hugh. She spoke of all her artist friends and how they strove to honour the talent they had been blessed with, despite the disinterest they encountered along the way. Most of her memories are happy ones, tinged with a sorrow for all those, now departed, who shared them with her. There were sad times too and you will read about them in the following pages, but I have been very aware, throughout the writing of this book, that I am only a medium through which Gladys has told her story. I can only tell what she has passed on to me and, although I have endeavoured to be as faithful as I can in relating all the facts she has given me, the truth is that this would have been an altogether more insightful book were she to have written it herself.

In writing a book such as this, the difficulty is always what to include and what to leave out. I began at the beginning - Gladys' birth - and have continued chronologically right down to the present day, detailing the major events and milestones in both her personal life and her career. I have included detail, but have been selective in doing so, as there are some events about which there exists a lot of documented material and, likewise, other events about which information is scant and, therefore, I have tried to spread the narrative evenly over the course of Gladys' life.

Along with the audio-tapes, Gladys gave over to me a vast amount of reference material; photographs, letters, catalogues, slides and scrapbooks. These scrapbooks - twenty in all - have been an invaluable source as their contents contain references to her which stretch right back to her schooldays in the 1920s. They run chronologically, and she has been meticulous in recording dates and sources, with almost no omissions. She has also pasted into them every article and review she herself wrote, for newspapers and magazines, during her career as art critic and fashion correspondent.

Central to the development of the book has been Gladys' own memory. Her ability to retain and recall the details of her life has been the pivot around which the basis of this book revolves, and without which it would never have come about. She is the possessor of a photographic memory and it is this ability that has allowed her to be so colourful in relating her memories.

I have written extensively about Gladys' paintings in previous publications and have decided, therefore, that this book should deal primarily with her life. It is not concerned with formal critique, rather, it is concerned with the human life story of a remarkable woman.

Without doubt, the inclusion of many photographs from Glady's collection has added greatly to the telling of her story and this book would be a far lesser volume without them.

Finally, and most importantly, I would like to thank Gladys for affording me the opportunity to tell her story. At all times, she has been most generous in giving of her time and most gracious in her praise when reviewing drafts. I can only hope that I have done her justice and that I have come some way in affording her the tribute she so richly deserves.

Susan Stairs
2004

Gladys as a baby in the arms of her mother, Elizabeth

ONE

With William's new position had come a house – Oakfield …

I remember the night I was born. I remember being very uneasy; and crying bitterly; and being carried about the room by two kind women… who I later knew to be my aunts, Julia and Daisy.

And I remember in the darkness, looking down at a bed and seeing someone in the bed… my mother, Elizabeth, though I did not know who she was at the time.

I had to get to know her and, indeed, all my relatives. I didn't understand anything except that I did not like the situation I was in. I didn't even know that I was human – or what that meant!
(Gladys Maccabe)

It was a warm night in June. For four years, the world had been at war; the Great War it was called, and great it was. Its effects had spread far and wide; crossing borders and continents, reaching into cities and towns and spreading across swathes of countryside to the smallest of villages, bringing great changes in its wake. Few places were immune to its force; not even the community of Randalstown in Co Antrim could escape. Many young men from the town enlisted with the Army and went off to the trenches, some never to return. Randalstown had become a base for the military and the town was full of young men in uniform. Nestling on the shores of Lough Neagh, it was a picturesque little place, but was, nonetheless, home to a thriving industry that was vitally important to the economy of the Province. At the time, Ulster had been associated with the production of linen for over

William Moore

one hundred and fifty years and produced cloth of the finest quality which was exported all over the world.

The Old Bleach Linen Company had been founded in Randalstown in 1864 by Charles James Webb. Resting in her room that night, having just given birth to a little girl, was Elizabeth Agnes, one of the daughters of William Moore, the Company's first manager and also its secretary for many years. In his younger days, William had studied flax and the linen business in Belfast Technical College and had gained the Queen's medal. Then, a chance meeting with one of the Webb family resulted in him being invited to manage their new factory in Randalstown. The town had been chosen as an ideal place to establish a linen factory because of the proximity of the river Maine which could provide a plentiful water supply. Also, there had always been a firm cottage weaving tradition in the area. Demand for linen was high, due in no small part to the American Civil War which had caused a shortage of cotton. The Old Bleach Linen Company supplied tableware to royalty and also to the dining rooms of the ships of the Cunard Line.

With William's new position had come a house – Oakfield – and he settled there with his young wife Martha. They had married when he was twenty-seven and she was just seventeen. William was Church of Ireland and Martha was Presbyterian and it is perhaps a testament to their respect for one another

The Moore family outside Oakfield around the turn of the last century. Back row, left to right; Parents William and Martha, Walter, Susan, William (Willie), Thomas. Middle, left to right; Julia, Olivia (Minnie), Herbert, Samuel, Elizabeth (Gladys' mother). Front, left to right; Margaret (Daisy), Frederick (Fred), Arthur, Alfred.

Martha Moore (nee Whiteside), Gladys' maternal grandmother, pictured just before her marriage – aged seventeen – to William.

Martha in later years.

– and their foresight – that they agreed between them that half of their children would be baptised in their father's faith and half in their mother's. If they had not come to this compromise, they perhaps would have had an argument about it some thirteen times, for, as time went on, Oakfield became home to their eight boys – Tom, Walter, Willie, Herbert, Alf, Sam, Arthur and Fred – and five girls – Susie, Minnie, Elizabeth, Julia and Daisy.

Theirs was a happy and loving childhood. Oakfield was comfortable and had the benefit of electricity – provided by the generator for the linen factory – which was certainly not commonplace in every house at the time. Martha and William's home was filled with music and song and a strong appreciation for art and literature.

William was known as an excellent scribe and was often called upon to write letters for those who had not been fortunate enough to learn how to take pen to paper. Both he and his wife were genial people who would have been well known and popular with those in the village. William was an enthusiastic golfer – he was a member of the Masserine Golf Club in Co. Antrim – and his many trophies were proudly displayed on shelves and mantles in Oakfield. Every evening, he smoked his last pipe while walking up the road with the local Catholic priest – the church and priest's residence being only about 500 yards from Oakfield. He possessed an excellent tenor voice that was heard on many a concert platform, and he played a number of instruments. Each of his children also learned to play and sing. It is little wonder that their home became known as a place of musical entertainment, with passers-by often lingering at the garden gate to listen to the music and song coming from within.

Martha was conscientious and energetic. When she was younger, she was often invited to open the ball – along with a prominent member of the Old Bleach Linen Company – at their annual dance. She was a very good dancer and a 'good looker' too and was, therefore, much in demand! She had studied dress design and was accomplished in drafting patterns and making her own clothes and those of her family. She was keen that her children should look presentable, neat and fashionable. Her daughters were always tastefully dressed and she also supervised her son's wardrobes, choosing the material for their suits. They would walk up and down in front of her in the room whenever they had had a new suit of plus-fours or whatever made for them, so that she could see if it had been properly tailored. Martha was by no means dictatorial, it was just that her family respected her taste and valued her judgement. As a young girl, she had often asked her brother, Tom, to take a sally rod down from the hedges for her. She would find an opening in the hem of her skirt and push the rod through it all the way around so that it stood out just like a crinoline – which was the height of fashion at the time. Then she would swish and spin around and around, showing off to her beloved brother. He died while he was still young and it broke her heart, but she kept his memory alive by naming her first son after him.

Another of her children lay on the bed that night during the war, cradling her own first born in her arms - a tiny new granddaughter for Martha. Elizabeth and her young husband, George, watched lovingly as their newborn baby girl looked around the room, taking in all that she saw and storing it away in her memory forever. They named their little girl Gladys and she was to be their only child. For Martha and her family it was indeed a momentous occasion, and one that they would, naturally, always remember.

Elizabeth and Gladys.

They did not expect, however, that the tiny addition to their family would recall her entrance into this world as well as they themselves would. For the little girl was blessed with a memory that was quite exceptional - a photographic memory indeed – and she is adamant today that she can recall the events of that night, all those years ago. She can remember being carried around the room by her aunts and seeing her mother lying on the bed. Gladys kept the memory of it inside her head for a long time before telling her mother, and when she did, Elizabeth smiled wryly, knowing so well that although it sounded impossible, she had no reason to doubt the conviction of her daughter.

She can remember lying in her pram...

Little Gladys Chalmers spent almost the first two years of her life in Randalstown. She was loved, cherished and probably spoilt by her large extended family. Her inquisitive mind noted and absorbed all that went on around her and she loved being surrounded by people, revelling in the comfort and security that they afforded. She can remember lying in her pram at Oakfield, and feeling such contentment as her aunts and uncles smiled down at her, speaking in soothing loving voices. But she can also remember the anxious cry of her mother as she caught her little girl chewing on a copying ink pencil she had managed to get her hands on one day while sitting up in her pram! Gladys says that there was rarely a time when she did not have a pencil in her hand – or in her mouth – and even as a very small girl she filled page after page with what she now realises were abstract patterns. And she was afforded every opportunity to use the talent which manifested itself so early on in her childhood.

'That is a violin, Gladys,' he told her… 'and this is a guitar.'

The love of music which has stayed with her all her life was also nourished in those early days in Oakfield. She remembers one day, while she was still a baby, one of her uncles gathering her up in his arms and carrying her around the room pointing out the musical instruments which lined a high shelf running around the walls. 'That is a violin, Gladys,' he told her as he lifted her up to see, 'and this is a guitar.' He named each one for her and she can remember being enthralled, even at such a tender age.

Her aunts Susan and Daisy both taught music and, over the years, many children and adults from all over the surrounding countryside and religious divide, learned to play the piano under their instruction at Oakfield. There were two pianos in different rooms and in one of the rooms there were two doors that faced each other. So as not to disturb any lesson which might be in progress, curtains were hung across the corner, making a small triangular space which blocked the room off from anyone who passed through it. Gladys would often stand in this little space and peep through the curtains unseen, so pleased that the person being taught was not herself!

Gladys would listen, enthralled, as her aunt played the piano…

Susan and Daisy also organised musical functions and plays for children and Susan, who was the quieter of the two, played the organ in the local church. She had been a teacher at one of the schools in the area, but had been invited by the then Lady O'Neill of Shane's Castle, near Randalstown, to become Organist and Choirmistress of the Parish church. Susan accepted the position and filled it for forty years. Gladys very often went with her while she practised the organ and found ways of amusing herself while her aunt played. She remembers running around the church, investigating every nook and cranny and sitting in the pews, pretending she was singing the hymns on a Sunday. She even climbed up to the pulpit and gave an impromptu sermon to the empty church a number of times! Although she enjoyed it, she felt, she says, a great reverence there and can remember the feeling to this day.

Daisy was the youngest of the Moore family. She had been christened Margaret but became forever known as Daisy ever since one of her brothers told her when she was little that she was just like 'a wee daisy'. Her fiancé at the time used to take her to all the popular musicals of the day, and she knew the musical scores to many of them. Gladys would sit, enthralled, as her aunt played the piano, relating the story to her as she went along. Martha was pleased that her little granddaughter was so interested in music and made sure that she received regular piano lessons from Susan and

Musical evenings and social gatherings were frequent at Oakfield…

Daisy. Gladys, however, wasn't so eager to sit and practice and would often try her best to find a way out of it! Martha often announced;
'You know, she hasn't had her finger on the piano for a fortnight!' That, in a house such as Oakfield, was considered to be the crime of crimes.

Musical evenings and social gatherings were frequent at Oakfield and, as a result, the Moore family were high on the party lists of their neighbours and friends. It was at one of these parties in Randalstown that Gladys – and the rest of her family – heard radio for the very first time:

Auntie Susie.

'Radio had just come in in those days. I was very small – I mustn't have been more than three or four… The earphones were passed around . . . my head was too tiny to hold them, so they were held up to one ear. I could hear this orchestra and I thought how wonderful it was that I could hear all those instruments being played in the room, even though I couldn't see any musicians actually playing them.'

Martha and her granddaughter became very close. Gladys had never known her grandfather, for William had died in 1913, five years before she was born. He had been ill for a time; and when he knew the end was near, he summoned his thirteen children to his bedside. Despite his weakness, he referred to each one by name, telling them how he wanted them to behave after he was gone. And he praised them all – his five daughters and eight sons – for having been such a loyal and loving family. Towards the end of her father's speech, Elizabeth could stand it no longer and she ran from the room in tears.

Auntie Daisy.

Elizabeth, far right, and Susan, far left. It is not known who the other two women are.

TWO

Elizabeth had inherited her mother's interest in art. She had a definite talent and all she had ever wanted to do was become an artist. So she studied art and eventually became an oil painter and a damask designer with The Old Bleach Linen Company. Indeed, her designs were used for many years. Her work there ceased, however, when she married, which would have been standard practice at the time. And how she met her husband is, as Gladys now says, an interesting story . . .

George Chalmers was a young Scot – from Aberdeen – who had arrived in Randalstown during the First World War. He was an officer in The Gordon Highlanders and his Regiment was stationed in Shane's Castle Park in the town. He had been gassed during the war already, having spent quite some time fighting in the trenches. So although he was only twenty-three, he had seen more of war than most of us are likely to experience.

He had some free time on his first day in Randalstown and was thus provided with an opportunity to wander around and explore the town, so he and a fellow officer set out to do just that. As they walked along, George happened to notice a girl on the opposite side of the street. He turned to his friend, remarking, 'Do you see that girl over there? I'd marry her tomorrow – if she'd have me.'

Elizabeth Moore – Gladys' mother.

Well, that girl was Elizabeth Moore and, at that time, she was pledged to a young officer who was out fighting at the front, so it is not surprising that she didn't notice the fellow who had spied her from across the street. Randalstown was full of military during that time, many regiments having been billeted there, but Elizabeth went about her business with barely a thought as to their presence.

George Chalmers – Gladys' father – as a cadet.

George, however, did not let this put him off, and he decided to do a little detective work. He discovered that the girl who had taken his fancy had a sister who played the organ at the local Church of Ireland and that Elizabeth often sang in the choir there. So smitten was he, that he began looking through one of the church windows at practice time – standing on a box – and watched Elizabeth as she sang. He also found out that she volunteered regularly for a charity organisation for the military. One evening, when he knew she would be there, he went in with the sole purpose of getting to know her. Elizabeth was serving tea and he proceeded to help her, handing back cups and being as useful as he could. But to her, he was just another soldier and she took no special notice of him.

However, he still persisted. One Sunday evening, a service for the military was held in the church. Elizabeth attended, along with her younger sister Daisy, and during the service, she looked across and thought she recognised a young man whom she had met in Portrush the previous year. 'Look, Daisy, there's George Muir,' she whispered to her sister beside her. 'We met him in Portrush last year, remember? He's from Scotland.' Daisy looked over and realised that she did indeed recall George Muir, and, after the service, both she and Elizabeth went up to the young man, asking him how he had come to be in Randalstown. Well, of course, George was delighted that the girl he had been so anxious to speak to for the past few weeks had approached him. So, even though he knew that she had quite obviously mistaken him for someone else, he said nothing about it for the time being.

Down the aisle of the church the three of them walked and Elizabeth listened as the soldier told her how he played the pipe organ and how hymns were intoned and about the different stops that were used in the organ and so on. And as she listened, she began to realise that his accent was quite different from that of George Muir. That young man had come from Glasgow and she remembered his distinctive way of speaking. But this young man was the absolute double of the person she and Daisy had met in Portrush. Puzzled, she looked closer at him.
'It is George Muir, isn't it?' Elizabeth asked the young man beside her. Poor George realised now that he had to come clean.
'Well', he admitted with a smile, 'It's George alright, but it isn't Muir, it's Chalmers actually, but does that matter?'
Poor Elizabeth nearly melted with embarrassment, for in those days, girls simply did not speak to a young man until he had first spoken to them and she realised with horror that it was she who had made the first approach. But

George, of course, was most thankful for this breach in etiquette and case of mistaken identity. As they reached the church door, he turned to Elizabeth. 'Allow me to carry your umbrella,' he offered with a smile, ' I'll walk you both home.'

Out into the night they went and along the snow covered paths. Elizabeth, still mortified at her mistake, did not speak the whole way home; instead, she listened to Daisy and George as they talked animatedly about their shared passion for music. Reaching the gate of Oakfield, they stopped and stood talking for a few moments. By now, Elizabeth was sure that the young man was quite taken with her sister. Of course, she could not know it was her he had thought about and watched – not Daisy – in the weeks since his arrival.

Towards the gate came Martha, along with her sister-in-law – the girls' aunt – who was always invited to supper on a Sunday evening. She saw her two daughters speaking to the young man in uniform and immediately found herself thinking about her own sons who were away at war. Five out of her eight boys had joined up and her thoughts turned to the day they had left for war. It was Elizabeth who had chased after Fred, the youngest of the boys, as he ran down the road, crying that he, too, wanted to go off to war, like his cousin, Billy, who was also his best friend. Fred was a year too young to join up, but that didn't stop him from trying.

'You'll break our mother's heart!' Elizabeth had called out to him.

Martha didn't know it at the time, but all five of her sons would survive the

'Off the South Stack at Holyhead' by Gladys' father, George Chalmers

war and, remarkably, return home uninjured. Billy, however, was not so fortunate. He was killed on his first day at the Front.

Martha now looked at some other mother's son who was chatting with her girls. He too was away from home, and although not in the thick of it now, was nonetheless deserving of some kindness and hospitality. And so, as the flakes of snow began to fall and the night's cold air closed in around them, she found herself at the gate, asking the young soldier, 'Won't you come in and have supper with us?'

George and Elizabeth in Portrush.

George wasted no time in accepting, for he felt at that moment as if he had been invited into heaven itself.

Once inside, the family learned that he – like them – was not only interested in music, but in art as well. He told them that he had been an illustrator working in black and white, and they also learned that he was an excellent calligrapher. At the girls' request, he wrote and drew in their autograph books and they, in turn, accompanied him on the piano as he sang his favourite songs for them. They also learned that his family was connected to the 18th century Scottish portrait artist, Sir George Chalmers (d.1791).

George's intentions towards Elizabeth became apparent soon enough. He managed to persuade her to end her relationship with the young man she had been pledged to and turn her entire attentions to him. So, the girl he had told his friend he would 'marry tomorrow' if she would have him, did indeed become his wife not so very long after that. They married in Randalstown, with George in full uniform, his fellow officers providing a guard of honour for the young couple outside the church.

George and Elizabeth got a house of their own in Randalstown after Gladys was born, but when she was about two years old, they decided to move to Belfast. Accommodation was scarce after the war, however, they managed to find a flat in Hopefield House which was off Kansas Avenue, staying there only a while before buying a house in nearby Willowbank Gardens on the Antrim Road.

Now George, as a result of having breathed mustard gas during his time in the trenches, was frequently ill, having to stay in bed for long periods of time. Gladys recalls him being bedridden at one point for a whole year. It can't have been easy for Elizabeth to have her husband so incapacitated, but George had his officer's pension for the three of them and this helped them on their way, along with their love for one another. Little Gladys was the light of their

He loved to read her stories – and she loved to listen.

Gladys, aged two, with her parents.

Gladys in her paternal grandfather's garden in Aberdeen, Scotland.

lives, and George looked forward to her running in from playing outside and settling herself down on the side of his bed. He loved to read her stories – and she loved to listen. Hans Christian Anderson was a favourite, but he would also tell her about all sorts of things, such as the origin of his name – Chalmers – how it derived from the Cameron clan, one of the ancient clans of Scotland. He would tell her how that clan was described as being 'fiercer than fierceness itself' and how, when he first had come face to face with war in the trenches, he hoped that he would have the courage to live up to the gallant name. He was always cheerful, even when he had to stay in bed. Visitors to the house often remarked on how much they themselves had been lifted after a chat with George.

During this time, while he was confined to bed, he was advised by his doctor to write down his experiences of the war. His pages, entitled *Wartime Reminiscences (1914-1918)* which Gladys has kept through all these years, describe how he decided, with his friend Alick, to enlist with the Territorial Forces while they were both still only young lads.

One evening, they had seen a mutual acquaintance with *'an important-looking leather belt over his jacket and a rifle slung over his shoulder.'* He told them he had joined the Territorials and was on his way to a rendezvous for an evening's drilling. He gave them a glowing account of the excitement to be found in the ranks of his battalion, and his words and appearance seduced George and his friend into joining up: *'We knew nothing of war or fighting, but were, rather, intrigued by the thought of getting into uniform and spending evenings in military training. The exuberance of youth would not be denied and we took the oath with little knowledge of its implication.'*

Those implications would become apparent soon enough when war broke out. Both boys were posted to France and endured the terror for much of the war. But if George's doctor was hoping that his patient might relive some of that terror on paper, perhaps for some cathartic effect, he was probably disappointed. For what George gives us in his writings is an amusing and sometimes very touching account of the many soldiers he served with; the scrapes they found themselves in and the happy times they shared despite their predicament.

He rarely has a bad word to say about any of them, and, instead of dwelling on the deaths of his fellow soldiers, he gives us detailed descriptions of their characters in life; their humour; their stubbornness; their loyalty and their courage. It is surely a testament to his own character – and also to the prevailing attitude of the time - that he emphasised the camaraderie he enjoyed at the front at the expense of describing the terrible suffering he endured.

Gladys had proven herself to be a bright and intelligent little girl and was very certainly loved and cherished by her parents. Her eyes observed all that went on around her and these things she saw, she would return to time and again much later on in her life when she needed inspiration for her painting.

She recalls being surrounded by her aunts and uncles and, although an only child, was never lonely, but would have loved to have had a brother or sister. Elizabeth, unfortunately, lost a baby when Gladys was about five years old. She suffered acute appendicitis and needed an operation, during the course of which she lost the child she was carrying, much to Gladys' regret.

Gladys played often with her cousin Beatrice – her Uncle Walter's daughter – both girls going to each other's houses, and seeing a lot of one another at their grandmother's house at holiday times as well. She had her own playroom at Willowbank Gardens, and in it was a little chemist's shop, complete with bottles of 'medicine', 'pills' and so on. She remembers playing with it 'for hours on end'. There were regular visits to Oakfield and a few trips to her father's home in Aberdeen, Scotland. Companionship also came from the succession of servants who helped with the chores in the house.

Often, Gladys would be taken to Alexandra Park to play and she remembers that the current girl would sometimes accompany the family when they took a box at the Belfast Hippodrome for the Christmas Pantomime.

She had her own playroom . . . and in it was a little chemist's shop.

There were oil paints and inks of all colours in the Chalmers' house. Gladys' father was fond of doing illuminated addresses which he decorated with gold leaf paint and coloured inks. Although her mother almost stopped doing any 'serious painting' while Gladys was growing up, she could never deny the talent she had been given. Often, as she sat by the fire, she would lift the poker and, on a little piece of wood, or on the top of a fig box, would do a little design in poker-work. Sometimes, she painted a picture and ornamented the frame with poker-work too. Decorating with any implement that came to hand, she was constantly making designs and patterns on pieces of furniture and the like. A little occasional chair would be painted red with a design on its back; there were many such examples in their home. Even in the dining room in Oakfield, there was a large overmantle, the frame of which Elizabeth had carved. On the sides of the glass, she had painted a scene of water birds sitting amongst reeds.

Once, Elizabeth had a little black silk coat made for Gladys. Her designer's fingers got to work on it and she painted the Greek key pattern in gold all around the collar and down the front. A milliner made a matching hat, complete with pink lining. It was most unusual for a child to be dressed in black at the time and little Gladys attracted a fair amount of attention whenever she wore it.

Elizabeth had a little black silk coat made for Gladys...

Gladys in her black silk coat, with her father.

THREE

Gladys would not learn of her father's experiences in the trenches during the Great War until she was older, but she was, nevertheless, to have some understanding of war at a very young age. The long history behind the conflict between the religions in Northern Ireland is one which Gladys has lived her own life through. Even at the young age of three, she was witness to the terror that comes from sectarianism; the awful result that derives from the belief that one is simply better than another.

Gladys was awakened…

Late one night, Gladys was awakened by the sound of her mother and father opening the door of her room. Their worried faces would have been noticed immediately by their perceptive child. Something was not right, she could tell, and she listened as they explained that they would have to move her bed. Apparently, shots had been fired over their house from another district and things were beginning to get very heated in the area. George and Elizabeth were terrified that a stray bullet might come through the window of their little girl's bedroom. So together, they shifted their daughter's bed out of line with the window. Gladys can remember how frightened she felt, her young mind trying to understand why she might not be safe in her own room – in her own bed – when it was the place she thought of as being the safest of all.

Because of the escalation of violence, a nightly curfew was soon imposed. If George and Elizabeth were entertaining in the evenings, supper had to be eaten earlier then usual so that friends could rush home safely before they were caught. Neighbours would sometimes stay over the time of the curfew, slipping later out of the back gate and along the dark silence to their own house, as quietly as they could, to avoid being seen.

The Chalmers' friends included two young Catholic brothers – one of them a solicitor - who played tennis regularly with George and Elizabeth. They enjoyed each other's company and would scarcely even have contemplated that this might result in the arrangement of an evil plan. But George learned later that, one evening, a group of men had been planning to burn his family out of their house. The Chalmers had not lived long in the area at the time and their religion would not have been certain to those people who were actually concerned with these things. But because they associated with the two brothers, it was assumed that they were Catholics also, and therefore a 'legitimate target'.

Sectarianism was rampant. Out on the streets, scenes witnessed by Gladys have remained with her all these years. She remembers walking along Antrim Road one morning, holding her mother's hand. Elizabeth wanted wool for a piece she was crocheting, so the two of them went into one of the shops to get some. They were there only a few moments when, suddenly, Gladys noticed that everybody had become very flustered. All around her, adults were whispering over her head and, again, she perceived correctly that something was wrong.

Elizabeth took her by the hand and made for the door. Just before they stepped outside, they learned that a man had been shot and killed on the street. He had been sitting at the front of his horse-drawn bread-cart along with a companion. Delivering bread to the shops was their only concern, but there were others who had a different plan for one of them. The spectators learned that one of the bread men was Catholic and the other Protestant. Gladys does not recall which of them was killed, but she does remember that the 'wrong one' was shot. Whoever fired the shot, ended up killing one of their own. The futility of it all was not lost on the very young Gladys, and it has lasted with her always.

Brookvale Collegiate School in Brookvale Avenue was chosen for Gladys and she started – as all children did in those days – at the age of six. A small, private girls' school, it was to provide her with ten years of education. It was run by a Miss Ferguson, whose family had been friends of Elizabeth's family in Randalstown; Miss Ferguson's father was Presbyterian minister there. It therefore seemed natural to enrol Gladys in the school as the two families had always been close. Also, music and art featured strongly on the curriculum in Brookvale, so it was ideally suitable for Gladys. She had developed such a strong interest in art that it was only natural her parents would try to encourage her in every way. She was still filling notebooks of every kind with abstract patterns which interested her far more than 'realistic' drawings or drawings of natural objects. And so, her first day at school arrived;

'I remember the first day I went into the kindergarten. I was quite nervous as a wee girl of six. The teacher asked me who I should like to sit beside and the first person my finger lit on was a girl called Pat Newell. Pat was a little older than me and I sat in the desk beside her. She was very kind to me in those first few days, until I got used to it all!'

Her years there were happy and industrious. She enjoyed tennis, hockey, music and drama - taking part in school plays, concerts, musical recitals and competitions. She also studied the piano, playing for morning prayers and accompanying the choir at choir lessons. School concerts were held in a hall in central Belfast, and Gladys played piano solos at these. But her favourite subject was, of course, art. Now that she was surrounded by people, Gladys' interest in them deepened. She used her friends and indeed all the girls in the school as subject matter, drawing portraits of them whenever she could. Lifelong friends were made in Brookvale – the Strain sisters, Margaret and Tom (christened Mary, but always called Tom after the uncle she so resembled when she was born) – and

Gladys (middle) with her best friends, Tom (left) and Margaret (right) Strain.

Gladys (extreme left) with Margaret (beside Gladys) and Tom (extreme right) performing a dance as part of the Windsor School of Dancing and Physical Culture's annual display in the Wellington Hall, Belfast, 1931.

Margaret sat at a desk with Gladys all the way through school. The three girls were inseparable, spending as much time together as they could.

George enrolled Gladys in a Presbyterian Sunday School. However, to her, it had none of the attractions of Brookvale, especially as none of her close friends attended. So, it was often the case, that on those Sunday afternoons when she was supposed to be enriching her young life with the study of all things divine, little Gladys could instead be found frolicking about the place with her friends, playing truant from Sunday School!
'This certainly did not please my father!' she says now.

Gladys' talent was developing strongly and it was becoming apparent that she was very gifted both artistically and musically, excelling in both areas at school. Every year, the girls in Brookvale were entered for The Royal Drawing Society Examinations. They were given prior notice of the Society's requirements for each examination and Gladys recalls with affection that special time in the school when everything was very quiet while each student did her work. Every year Gladys sat the exam, and every year she reached the grade.

Elizabeth and George's daughter's success was a source of joy to them, especially as they themselves had similar talents. They watched as Gladys' skill developed and they constantly encouraged her. George probably wished that his health was better than it was so that he could take a more active part in encouraging his daughter and Gladys remembers him saying to her when she was about ten years old;
'One day now, I must take you to the Art Gallery.'

Memory of James Humbert Craig 1877 - 1944

His own interest was as keen as his daughter's. He knew a few of the artists who lived in Belfast at the time and stopped to chat with them whenever he was able to be out and about. One of them was James Humbert Craig (1878-1944) and Gladys can remember seeing him going around the town. He looked, she says, like 'a ball of tweed' because he wore a heavy tweed suit and a tweed hat which was always stuck with fish flies. Colin Middleton (1910 –1983) she remembers from that time also. He always had a paint box and a palette under his arm as he passed by the Chalmers' house on his way to visit a friend who lived nearby.

Gladys waited patiently, and sure enough, the day came when her father was well enough to take her to the newly built Belfast Museum and Art Gallery in Botanic Gardens (now the Ulster Museum). It had only just opened its doors that year – 1929 – and Gladys was more than excited. George was unable to drive his car on account of his illness, so they took two trams to get from Antrim Road to Stranmillis. There was a huge expectation on Gladys' part and the events of the day are strong in her memory, not least because it would become one of the last outings she would ever have with her father.

As soon as she walked into the rooms of the beautiful new Gallery, Gladys

'If I could ever paint like that!'

knew at once what she wanted to do when she grew up. If there had ever been any doubt in her young mind as to what her destiny would be, it was dispelled that day as she wandered through the rooms gazing up at the work of so many masters of painting. She was going to be an artist. Her mind was made up.

'I was absolutely thrilled with all these paintings. I thought it would be marvellous to be an artist'

Belfast born Sir John Lavery (1856-1941) had presented thirty-four of his own works to the new Gallery, and, after a while, Gladys and her father came upon his self-portrait hanging in one of the rooms. They both stood in front of it for some time and Gladys recalls that she was spellbound.

'Oh Daddy!' she whispered. 'If I could ever paint like that!'

George had her by the hand and his grip tightened when he heard her wistful little voice. Still fixed by Lavery's gaze, he squeezed her hand even harder and spoke to her with conviction;

'One day, Gladys,' he told her 'you will have a painting hanging in this gallery.'

She had no reason to doubt him; his belief in her told her that his words would come true.

But George's health was still poor. The gas he had breathed while in the trenches had damaged his lungs so much that he still had to spend large amounts of time resting in bed. Often, when he needed a lot of attention, Gladys was simply taken out of school and sent to Randalstown, for in those days, schools were not obliged to have constant attendance of pupils. She loved the freedom of being out in the country and had many hours to play on her own. There was a swing out the back, hanging between two cherry trees,

Gladys loved to venture out by herself to the moss

and she would sit on it for hours, making it fly as high as she could. Her youngest uncle, Fred, was very good to her. They would compete against each other on the putting green on the lawn and he took her for runs on the bar of his bicycle. He had great patience and never lost his temper, even when Gladys teased him – which she was more than happy to do! Fields were next to the house and she often spent an afternoon riding her bicycle along their well-worn paths. Also, she would play in her little 'vegetable shop' at the back of the house, which consisted of a long piece of wood placed on two lines of bricks at either end. Aunts and Uncles 'bought' scallions and cabbages - and whatever other green things that might resemble vegetables - which she had gathered from the garden.

About two miles along the road lay the 'moss', which was where the turf was cut. At one time her grandfather, William, had purchased a small moss for his own use and turf was delivered to Oakfield in a horse-drawn cart and piled up high in one of the outhouses. Gladys loved to venture out by herself to the moss. In the early mornings, she would cycle out and sit there in the silence. It was the atmosphere – the quietness and the solitude - and the landscape of the place that attracted her.

On a sunny evening at Oakfield, Gladys nestles into her Auntie Daisy's fox fur to have her picture taken with the ladies before they embark on a trip. Also pictured are Elizabeth (far left) and Auntie Julia.

FOUR

In 1930, it was almost twelve years since the war had ended and George had been bed bound for an entire year. As a result, he developed gallstones and was often in great pain. So it was decided that he should undergo an operation to remove them and preparations were made for him to be admitted to The Royal Victoria Hospital. Elizabeth wanted to be there for her husband, so Auntie Julia was summoned from Randalstown in order to look after Gladys.

Gladys with her cousins Hubert and Beatrice - in the front garden of Oakfield with Aunt Julia c. 1931.

The operation would be even more difficult for George than normal because the damage to his lungs meant that a general anaesthetic could not be administered. He was to have a local one instead. Gladys was excited at the prospect of having Auntie Julia staying over to mind her and she let George and Elizabeth go to the hospital without ever even dreaming that her life would never be the same again.

Gladys loved her Auntie Julia – no more than any of her other aunts – but Julia was such great fun, always making jokes and dressing up for amusement. She enjoyed sport, playing both golf and tennis and was involved in many of Randalstown's social activities. Like her sister Susie, Julia never married, but she had been engaged twice. The first time was to a school headmaster, but Julia broke off the engagement, against the wishes of her fiancé. The second engagement was to a young lawyer, when Julia was teaching in England. It ended, unfortunately, when the young man died suddenly during the influenza epidemic of 1918, and she remained single for the rest of her life. She returned from England when Martha became too elderly to head the family which, since the war ended, had been greatly reduced, many of her siblings settling in Canada and America and the others either married or living in their own homes.

With Julia there to entertain Gladys that night, any worries the little girl might have had about her father were put to the back of her mind. So, when it was time for bed, Gladys was tired out from all the fun and quickly fell asleep. Julia followed soon after. There was little point in staying up until Elizabeth came home, as it would probably be quite late by the time she felt able to leave her husband's side. So Julia slipped into the spare bedroom and fell asleep.

Auntie Julia acting as a fortuneteller, beside her 'tent' in the garden at Oakfield, to Gladys and her cousin Hubert – who were both also dressed up for the occasion – in 1932.

It was Gladys who was awakened in the middle of the night by loud knocking on the front door. She instinctively threw back the covers of her bed and left its cosiness to walk to the room where she knew Julia would be asleep. The knocking continued as she shook her aunt awake and watched as Julia rose and, instantly alert, went quickly downstairs to investigate. As her aunt trod on each step downwards, she probably knew in her heart that such a disturbance could only indicate bad news.

Gladys had followed her aunt out of the bedroom but had not ventured downstairs. She preferred to let Julia find out what all the fuss was about and so she waited on the landing even though her warm bed beckoned. The knocking grew louder as Julia reached the hall. Turning the key to open the inner door, she suddenly remembered that she had locked this door and the outer door as well. Whoever was so frantically banging to be let in must have broken through the glass on this door.

Upstairs, Gladys stepped closer to the bannister as she heard the knocking stop and someone almost falling into the hall. She went right up to the rail and leaned over it as far as she could, straining to hear the voice that was trying its best not to reach her ears. But it was only a matter of seconds before she realised that it was her mother; and no time at all before she knew that something was very wrong. She crept back into her room as the whispers and the crying moved closer and closer. It was something bad and it was coming upstairs. Round the door came Julia and Elizabeth, their faces white and their eyes red from tears. They took her in their arms and told her that her Daddy was gone. The three of them hung on to each other and cried and cried. Gladys, amid all the terrible sadness, remembers being astonished at seeing her Auntie Julia cry.

The explanations came, but would only be understood by Gladys later. Her father had needed a blood transfusion, but not enough of his blood type was available. Elizabeth offered to give some of her own, but was told by the doctor that it would not be suitable. As a result, George did not survive the operation. Elizabeth was given her husband's clothes and a taxi was called to drive her home. It must have been the longest and most dreadful journey she had ever taken. All her hopes and dreams of a long and happy life with the man she loved were now but dust to the wind. George was only thirty-six; they had had a mere thirteen years together. He would never see their little girl grow into a young woman; never listen to her breathless tales of

'Now you are the only one your mother has. You have to take the place of your father…'

excitement from school again; never smile to himself as he waited for her to flop onto his bed and plead for another story. But their little girl would make him proud; Elizabeth was sure of that.

The funeral was arranged and George's father travelled to Belfast from Aberdeen with his eldest daughter, Auntie Elizabeth. Gladys had always regarded her grandfather as quite a character - he was rather fond of the ladies, it was said – and he had also been something of a spendthrift. His wife – Gladys' grandmother – had died before Gladys was born. She had been the daughter of a dairy farmer who owned a prosperous business in the north of Scotland. Gladys' grandfather was choirmaster at a large Presbyterian church in Aberdeen and Gladys remembers seeing him conducting the choir on one of her trips there and also taking them all to the Highland Games in the car when she was very small. George and himself had not seen eye to eye over many things, but even so, it cannot have been easy for him to bury his son.

In those days, Gladys recalls, women did not attend funerals. They grieved at home, leaving the men to send their loved ones on their final journey. The day her father was buried, Gladys' grandfather came back to her house. He summoned her upstairs to the playroom and with all the tactfulness he possessed, sat her down and spoke to her.

'Your father is dead,' he told her. 'I saw him in his coffin and, you know, he looked very well in his white shirt and dark suit.' He fixed his gaze on hers. 'Now, you are the only one your mother has. You have to take the place of your father and you must always look after her.'

How daunting his words must have been to his eleven-year-old granddaughter. But they made a distinct impression on her and she has remembered them exactly to this very day.

George Chalmers 1892-1930.

Having declined an offer to go to live with George's family in Scotland, Elizabeth knew she had to bring some semblance of normality back into their lives – if only for the sake of her little girl. She was fortunate in that she had her own large and supportive family to call on for help if it were needed. She must have thought about her own father's death and how it had affected her. But William had lived a full life; he had fathered thirteen children; seen most of them grow, and, at least, had the reassurance that the older ones would take care of their mother and their younger siblings. George had been so young and it had been so sudden and unfair. Now Elizabeth was a widow, just like

At the tennis court in Randalstown. From left; Gladys, aged about eight years, Auntie Julia, Auntie Daisy and Auntie Elizabeth – one of Gladys' father's sisters from Scotland.

her mother, and she determined that her daughter's future would not suffer as a result. She could never stem the pain, but she would do whatever she could to help Gladys realise her dreams.

It was never going to be easy, Elizabeth knew that. The first obstacle came quite soon after George died. Contented as she had been that her late husband's pension would provide for the two of them, she was shaken when she realised that she should never have taken it for granted. It seems that because George's immediate cause of death was the operation for gallstones (and this was written on his death certificate), it was not taken into consideration that the gallstones were contracted as a result of his lengthy confinement to bed. This confinement, in turn, was due to the fact that he had been gassed during the war and his lungs badly affected. The authorities in question did not design it essential that his wife and child should be provided for after he died. The pension he had died with him it seems. The house and its furnishings were the only things of substance that Elizabeth owned. They would have the comfort of knowing they would have a roof over their heads, at least. Not long before he died, George had arranged to buy a site on which to build a new house at Chichester Park, further along Antrim Road, but it was not to be.

Mother and daughter remembered what George had always told them in his lilting Scottish accent;
'Don't worry too much about your life,' he had advised. 'You'll be looked after. The Lord always looks after us.'

Help came from the family, of course, and later, a young man called Jack Anderson went to live with Gladys and her mother as a paying guest. Jack was a friend of Gladys' Uncle Herbert in the Northern Bank head office in Belfast. A fine vocalist, pianist and organist, he was often invited to sing solo at concerts and similar entertainments. On these occasions, he invited Gladys to go along with him as his piano accompanist. As much as he enjoyed staying with the Chalmer's, so they enjoyed having him and Gladys recalls with pleasure the times they all spent together. Jack went to live in Portstewart when he retired, but Gladys kept in touch with him, and his sister, Ethel, who lived in Coleraine, visiting often, and she recalls how he referred to their house in Willowbank Gardens as 'a temple of the arts'!

Gladys had always been fond of her Uncle Willie, her mother's brother. Willie had never married. He had been engaged once, but, like his sister Julia's engagement, it came to an end when his fiancee died in the great flu epidemic of 1918 and he had never looked at another girl. After his brother-in-law died, he took it upon himself to almost 'adopt' his little niece. She needed a father, and he did his best to care for her as if she were his own. Gladys speaks of him with fondness:

'Then there was my mother's brother, my Uncle Willie. I'll never forget him. When my father died he seemed to sort of adopt me. He had a very hearty laugh. He was a tall, slim man; he looked like an army major – he had that sort of appearance. He was very popular. I don't think he had any guile in him whatsoever.'

Jack Anderson.

Gladys and her mother in the garden at Oakfield with cousins Austen and Beatrice and their Mother, Auntie Agnes.

Snowballing in the garden at Oakfield with Grandmother Martha and Aunts Daisy and Julia.

Willie was very musical and blessed with a confidence that allowed him to sit down at the piano and accompany himself while he sang, no matter the size of the audience. He was also a member of the Philharmonic Choir. At weekends, he would come to Belfast and take Gladys to the Opera or to a concert. Uncle and niece shared a love of music and Willie was adamant that he would bring a little light and laughter into Gladys' life. He knew he could never replace her father, but he would do his best to make her smile. At Oakfield, he and Gladys would often sit in a quiet room where he would read Shakespeare, Dickens and other authors to her.

Willie was very musical.

Willie took Gladys to a production of Peter Pan when she was twelve. It was nothing short of magical to the little girl. The title role was played by Jean Forbes Robertson – 'the definitive Peter Pan' - who played the part for nine seasons in the West End. Gladys was absolutely fascinated by the character that she played and how she played it. Newly developed at the time was the mechanism whereby actors could fly about the stage and, it being Peter Pan, there was plenty of flying to delight the audience. The whole event left a lasting impression on Gladys and she returned home full of tales about what she had seen. Uncle Willie was staying with his sister and niece that weekend and listened with pleasure to Gladys as she told everyone about the wonder of Peter Pan flying around the stage.

The next day, Uncle Willie went out for a while. On his return, he called Gladys to him and said he had a surprise for her. She looked at the piece of paper he presented her with and in an instant she saw that it was Jean Forbes Robertson's autograph. Willie had found out that the actress was staying at The Grand Central Hotel in Belfast and had slipped out and gone there, asking to see her. She had kindly given him her autograph and he had tucked the precious piece of paper into his pocket, beaming with pride all the way home. He could hardly wait to hand it to Gladys and see the look on her cute face. He wasn't disappointed. Gladys says that she

'was absolutely overwhelmed with delight. I never forgot about that; it was wonderful. And when I hear of Peter Pan, or see the play advertised, I always think of Uncle Willie and his kindness.'

Gladys' interest in art was increasing all the time. She was rarely without a drawing instrument of some kind in her hand whenever she had a spare moment. Throughout her teenage years, she developed her talent through constant practice and, at school, her efforts did not go unnoticed. She continued – as did all the pupils in Brookvale – to sit the Royal Drawing Society Examinations every year. At sixteen, she was the only Irish student to have a drawing reproduced in the Society's magazine. During her last year at the school, she was rewarded with the news that she had reached the Top Grade in the Examinations. Here was proof at last that she had a very special gift. Not that such proof were needed; but, to a young girl, an official verification of talent seems always to be worth that bit more than the everyday reassurances of a relative or friend. But there was an even more solid confirmation to come.

Miss Ferguson took the letter in her hands and looked up at the young girl waiting anxiously in front of her.

Gladys was summoned to the Principal's room one day. She wondered what it was Miss Ferguson needed her for, but she entered the room with only the slightest hesitation, for whatever it was, she knew that Miss Ferguson would communicate it in the nicest possible way. The Principal of Brookvale was a just and kindly woman and her nature had been underlined to Gladys even further in the time since her father had died. Gladys' parents had chosen the school for their daughter mainly for its emphasis on the arts and they were happy to pay to ensure that their daughter had the education which was most suited to her. This proved more difficult when George died, however. But Elizabeth never complained about the fees and, Gladys says,

'...*knowing her, she believed they would come from somewhere!*'

Each time the end of term came, all the girls were handed a small, white envelope with their school account, which was to be given to their parents. Gladys recalls:

'At the end of term just after my father's death, I was handed the little envelope like the other girls. When I took it home to my mother, she opened it, but the only amount it showed owing was the small entrance fee to a music examination! My mother was never again charged for my tuition at Brookvale and this practice continued until I left school at almost seventeen.'

Now, in Miss Ferguson's room, Gladys sat down and Miss Ferguson smiled at her, casting her warm eyes down to a letter which was sitting on her desk. She took the letter in her hands and looked up at the young girl waiting anxiously in front of her.

'Gladys,' she began, 'I have received some correspondence from The Royal Drawing Society.'

She could see that she had Gladys' interest immediately and she smiled as she continued, her downcast eyes scanning the lines of the page in her hand. She paused for a moment so that greater emphasis would be placed on the words she was next about to speak.

'They say that out of all the schools in the country whose pupils sit their exams, one pupil – who has reached the top grade - has particularly impressed the examiners.' Miss Ferguson put the letter down on the desk and looked up at Gladys.

'That pupil is you, Gladys!' she exclaimed. 'And, not only are they most impressed, they have invited you to go to their schools in London to study! Oh Gladys, isn't that wonderful?' she beamed. 'Such an opportunity! To be able to study art in London - it's what you've always wanted!'

Miss Ferguson's delight was so visible – and so obviously genuine – that Gladys felt obliged to smile. It was an honour indeed and inside she felt so

Brookvale Collegiate School first XI Hockey Team. Gladys is pictured fourth from right.

proud, so fortunate to have been singled out in this way. She could see how pleased the Principal was and the last thing she wanted was to disappoint her. But Miss Ferguson could sense Gladys' hesitancy.
'It is, Gladys…' she asked, '….what you've always wanted?'
'Well……yes. Yes, I suppose it is,' Gladys answered, trying her very best to be enthusiastic. If the truth were known, she would love to go to London. It would be wonderful. But there were other things – things that would always be of uppermost importance to her.
'You suppose it is?' Miss Ferguson was bewildered. 'Gladys, my dear, whatever is the matter? You have such a talent. You are so gifted. Do you think you do not deserve to go?'
Gladys looked down at the floor as she tried to find words to explain her feelings to her Principal. She thought about the words of encouragement her father had given her - his belief in her and her talent - and she thought about how much she missed him. She thought, too, about her own dear mother and how much they would miss each other were she to go to London.
'I realise it's such an honour, Miss Ferguson,' she replied. 'Really I do. And it's not that I don't appreciate it. And I do want to study art, but…….I can't go, Miss Ferguson…….not to London.' She brought her eyes up to meet those staring at her from across the desk. 'I could never leave my mother, you see. With my father gone, there are only the two of us and I could never leave her on her own. Even if she wanted me to go, I wouldn't.'
Miss Ferguson looked at the young girl opposite to her and nodded her head in silence. She wouldn't argue. She wouldn't try to change her mind. She knew Gladys would not be for turning and, she admired her for that. For one so young, she had such a strong mind; an unselfish one too.
'Well. I can't say that I'm not disappointed, Gladys,' she said with a sigh. 'It would have been such an opportunity for you. However, I understand your reasons and I must say that they are most admirable.' She folded the letter and, putting it back in its envelope, she rose from her chair.
Gladys stood up. 'Thank you Miss Ferguson,' she said. 'I knew you would understand.'

As she walked back to class, she had no sense of disappointment at having turned down the offer. Rather, she felt a great sense of opportunity. She believed in Divine guidance. She realised she always had. Whatever happened, happened for a reason. What her father had told her was right – The Lord looks after us. This was not a door closed, but a door opened. There was something else in store for her and she knew it wouldn't be long until she found out what it was.

Gladys aged about fourteen, with her Grandmother Martha.

When she heard what Gladys had done, Elizabeth was even more proud of her daughter. While she was disappointed for her, she knew that she had made up her own mind. Elizabeth would not try to change it. But it made her all the more determined to ensure that Gladys would go on to study art. If not in London, then in Belfast - at the Belfast College of Art. Elizabeth made enquiries, and soon she was answering any queries from friends or relatives as to the course her daughter's life would take after she left school with the confident riposte:
'Gladys is going to the College of Art'.

If her words were met with a disapproving look or a disparaging remark, she didn't mind. She had been fortunate to have been able to use her own talent when she was a young girl – when she had been an oil painter and a damask designer at the Old Bleach Linen Company with the full encouragement of her own parents– and she was adamant that her child would develop the talent which had been bestowed upon her. George would have wanted it too, she was certain of that. After all, he had been an artist as well. She would do anything she could to ensure that Gladys would go on to study art. They would find the means somewhere.

But Belfast was an unforgiving place in those days when it came to personal expression and artistic endeavour. It simply wasn't acceptable to many that a

Gladys, aged fourteen, with her Mother and Auntie Julia, in the centre of Belfast.

young lady should attend art college. What good could come from it? Surely young Gladys should be thinking about a sensible career, one that would provide for herself and her mother? Surely she had a duty to her late father to look after the both of them? What provision for the future could paints and canvas afford? It was nonsense, they would say, selfish nonsense.

However, the idea was firmly planted in Gladys' mind, despite anyone else's misgivings. She told Miss Ferguson, who was most pleased. Perhaps, she thought, Gladys' decision not to take up the offer of a place at The Royal Drawing Society's School had been the right one. Better to be among friends than strangers. Her young pupil was very close to her extended family and she knew how lonely she would have been in the big city of London. But she would not be without her detractors, Miss Ferguson was sure of that. Art was at the bottom rung of the ladder in relation to possible career options, and there would be many who would try to dissuade her.

In due course, some of George's acquaintances came to Elizabeth to advise her as to what plan of action she should take to ensure

Elizabeth, as drawn by Gladys in 1936.

that her daughter choose a suitable career. They were probably only looking out for their late friend's widow and her child, but if they thought they could influence the decision of either of them, they were to be disappointed.

One day, they delivered a message to the Chalmers' household to the effect that Mr So-and-So, an influential man in the city, (Gladys can not now remember his name, although it is doubtful she would divulge it even if she could!) had requested a meeting with Gladys at his grand house in South Belfast. Elizabeth and her daughter were curious. They didn't know the gentleman, but it would have been rude to decline the invitation and perhaps he had some information that could be useful to Gladys and her mother. And so, as Elizabeth got ready to accompany Gladys to his house one afternoon, she was hopeful that, on their return, Gladys might be a little wiser as to the course her life might take once she left Brookvale.

On their arrival at the house, they were ushered into a large drawing room, expecting they would be graciously received. Gladys looked around the room and saw that the man of the house was looking directly at her. Big and stout, he was sitting on a chaise-lounge, covered with a leopardskin rug.
'Now! I want to talk to you, young lady! I want to talk some sense into you!' he bellowed, without even greeting either of his guests. Before she could even begin to be surprised, he was booming again.
'Don't listen to that silly woman,' he said, dismissing Elizabeth with a wave of his hand. 'She's permitting you to study art, is she? What sort of a mother is that? I would rather my daughters would black boots than study art!' he spat.
Gladys could barely believe what she was hearing. That was her dear mother he was talking about in such a disparaging manner. Her dear mother, who had sacrificed so much on her daughter's behalf.
'Now you listen to me, young lady,' he continued. 'You will go and learn typing and shorthand and get a sensible job! Make some money for yourself and your mother.'
He was still staring at Gladys, expecting her to humbly bow before him and whisper 'Yes, Sir. Of course, Sir.' But the young girl in front of him was having none of it. Black boots indeed! she thought. How dare he! How could he speak to her like that? How could he demean her mother in such a horrible manner? She rose up from her chair, and, diminutive though she was, stretched herself up to her full height and announced;
'Mother! We're leaving.'

They both walked towards the door, and as they did, they heard him shout after them;

'You remember what I say!'

As soon as they stepped outside, Gladys burst into tears. She was so hurt that her mother had been so insulted. Elizabeth put her arm around her daughter's shoulder and told her they were going for a walk along the Lagan Boulevard. All the while, Gladys was crying bitterly and Elizabeth was trying to reassure her.

'Don't take any notice of that man, Gladys,' she told her daughter. 'Don't let him worry you. He certainly doesn't concern me. Don't upset yourself. I know what you want to do – and you will do it. I will see to it.'

The incident left a marked impression on Gladys and she didn't get over it for a long time. She informed Miss Ferguson about it, and she was very upset. She told Gladys that she would see if anything could be done about the obnoxious man, but no more was ever heard about it.

Soon after, Elizabeth made an appointment for Gladys and herself at the Belfast College of Art, which in those days was situated above the Belfast Technical College. They met with Professor Beaumont and Gladys

'I would rather my daughters would black boots than study art!'

remembers him as being most kind to them both. Elizabeth was anxious that he be told of their circumstances and Professor Beaumont devised a course for Gladys which would be financially suitable. Its accent was on design, painting, sculpture and fashion drawing.

When she left Brookvale, after ten happy years, Gladys began her course in the Belfast College of Art. Despite the misgivings of many, she had chosen her path and was determined to stay on it. But there was one person she knew she had to thank, for without her generosity and encouragement, she might not have even been able to finish school, let alone begin a college education.

Gladys tells how she went back to Brookvale:
'After I left school, I went down one day and asked to speak to Miss Ferguson. I was ushered into the sitting room (which was usually forbidden to pupils) and I sat down. When Miss Ferguson opened the door to enter, I, of course, immediately stood up and she welcomed me with a handshake and sat down. I sat on my chair and said,
'Miss Ferguson, I have come to thank you for what you have done for me since my father died.' And then I went on to tell her about Art College and what I was doing there. She said she was pleased that I was studying art, hoped that I was keeping up my music, asked about my mother and spoke generally. Then she turned meaningfully to me and said (as she lifted up her glasses and wiped a tear from her eye, which to me was so unlike our Headmistress) 'Gladys, you're the only girl who has ever come to thank me for anything and I do appreciate it.'
I have never forgotten this. Perhaps because it reminds me that gratitude requires to be spoken as well as felt.'

Strolling down Belfast's City Street in 1938; Gladys and her friend Tom Strain (later Tom Reynolds).

FIVE

Gladys was only seventeen years old when she first entered the Belfast College of Art in 1935. She had grown into a stylish and very pretty young lady. Her interest in art was coupled with an interest in fashion, and like her grandmother Martha, she designed and made many of her own clothes. With her fair hair and dark eyes, she would have been instantly spotted by the young man she met one day while walking into town to college. But closer inspection on his part revealed that the young lady was, in fact, someone with whom he had been acquainted when he was only a little boy. This was Gladys Chalmers, who, he now recalled, had lived quite near to him. They used to play together as children when he lived in the next avenue, Rosemount Gardens. And now, here she was, all grown up and quite sophisticated.

Max Maccabe, aged about eighteen years.

Gladys, for her part, remembered the young man too. He was Max Maccabe, one year older than herself and not only had they played together, but he had always chosen her in games as his partner. She had thought him handsome then, and, looking at him now, realised she still did. But it was the first time, she noted, that she had seen his hair, because, as a little boy, he always wore his Inst (The Royal Belfast Academical Institution) cap His mother, apparently, had told him that he must never take his cap off when playing outside – except to lift it to a lady, of course - and he had always obeyed, pulling it right down over his eyes.

Because they hadn't seen each other for quite a few years, the two of them began chatting about this and that, and Max found himself accompanying Gladys on her walk. She told him that she was now a student in the College of Art and was enjoying it very much. He told her he was in the insurance industry; working for the Fine Art & General Company. He was responsible for taking care of the insurance cover of works of art in private and public ownership. During the course of the conversation, he slipped in a little request:

Gladys in her late teens.

'Do you think you might like to come to the pictures with me one evening, Gladys?' he asked.

Gladys didn't have to think about her reply. She liked Max – she always had done. It was if she had known him all her life – in fact she very nearly had.

'That would be very nice,' she told him with a smile.

Not so very long after that, Max asked Gladys to go to a dance with him at The Floral Hall in Bellevue, which was the great dancing place at the time. Gladys loved to dance. Whenever she stayed in Randalstown, Aunt Julia and Uncle Willie would take her with them to the local dances at the golf and tennis clubs. Gladys admits today that she was probably far too young - she remembers all the older men dancing with 'this wee girl' – but her aunt and uncle were good chaperones and they loved to see her enjoying herself. Max's next invitation was to a dress dance at Belfast Castle. It was a very formal affair – the men in tailcoats, the women in beautiful long gowns – and Gladys loved the sheer spectacle. All the elements she admired were combined there; music, style, colour, fashion and crowds of people, and she thoroughly enjoyed herself. Even today, she paints ballroom scenes, recording pictures of a place and time she loved, now lost forever.

Max's next invitation was to a dress dance at Belfast Castle . . . the men in tailcoats, the women in beautiful long gowns . . .

Gladys' friendship with Max continued. She was now fully immersed in her course at the College of Art where she began to meet like-minded people who were just as interested in art as she was. Her fellow students and teachers alike she remembers clearly.

Newton Penprase (1888-1978) was a small, very pleasant man who taught pattern design and plan and elevation. At the time, he was in the process of building an unorthodox-style house on the North Antrim coast. At weekends, some of his students would arrive down at the site to help with bricklaying, plastering and so on.

Then there was Edward Marr. Gladys recalls:

'... a very refined Scotsman who arrived at the college during my time there. He was fair-haired and fair- moustached and quite a number of the girls fancied him. But he, apparently, only had eyes for one of them and she eventually became his wife. I remember one of the national newspapers at the time had the heading above the report of their marriage; 'Now he's her Lord and Master!' '

Gladys was in Edward Marr's classes at the College and she credits him with having taught her how to draw trees:

'I told him once, years later, at one of Mercy and George McCann's parties on Botanic Avenue that it was he who really made me see trees. That he – Edward Marr - had told me to always remember how branches grow on trees; they seem to emerge gracefully from the trunk. I told Edward that I could never paint a tree

Mr Mansfield, lecturer on Painting at Belfast College of Art, as depicted by Gladys in 1937.

without thinking of his remarks many years before. He was pleased and said, 'Hearing something like this makes the years I spent in art lecturing seem worthwhile.''

Naturally, life drawing formed part of the syllabus at the College of Art. Taking the life class at the time was Seamus Stoupe (1872-1949). He was,

Memory of Seamus Stoupe 1872–1949

The life-drawing class itself provided the students with a little quandary

Gladys now recollects, a very handsome, elderly man with white hair, always dressed in a well-cut tweed suit. On one occasion in his class, Gladys did a little sketch of him. As he passed behind her, he saw what she was doing and immediately recognised himself.
'If you would spend your time drawing the model instead of your teacher, it would be more to your benefit,' he remarked. But Gladys could see that rather than being offended, he was in fact quite pleased with his pupil's characterisation of him!

The life drawing class itself provided the students with a little quandary (well, the female students, at least) in that differing modes of modesty appeared to be conferred on the two sexes. Gladys – and her many girlfriends at the college - always found it unfair that while a male model was permitted to wear a loincloth, a female model had to pose completely naked. She says:
'they should either have covered her up in part or . . . well . . . I'll not go into the other!'

Fred Allen, later Art Critic for The Belfast News Letter, began teaching at the College of Art while Gladys was there. A tall, dark, young man, he seemed quite shy at first; Gladys supposes that he had probably just graduated himself. He seemed, she says, to be very in tune with the students and, on one occasion, was able to tell which one had painted which picture by 'reading' their characters from their painting.

Fashion design was taught by a Mrs Sloan. On one occasion, some adjudicators from a college in London travelled over to look at the students' work. Gladys had made a white corduroy suit, first drawing her idea then creating the pattern, selecting the fabric and sewing it together. The students were required to model their own design for the panel of judges and Gladys' suit was considered to be the best.

Gladys was enjoying her time at the College immensely. The subjects she was studying provided her with a growing knowledge of the art world and opened her eyes, not only to the many facets of an artist's life, but also to the difficulties they faced in an atmosphere of indifference. Art exhibitions were few and far between in the Belfast of the 1930s. Living artists were afforded almost no specialist venues in which to display their work. A small section in a department store was usually the only hanging space open to the artist in those days. It is difficult and, indeed, very sad, to think that many of those painters whose work is so sought after today, had so much of a struggle to even exhibit - never mind sell - their paintings. It is surely worthy of mention that these people sacrificed so much for the sake of their art. Were it not for that struggle, it is doubtful that we would have such a burgeoning art market today. The fruits of their talent are with us still - look through any current art auction catalogue in the country and work by these artists, at ever increasing estimates, can be seen.

What if they had decided that it was simply no use; that there was no point in painting any more because so few were appreciative? It can be said that there will always be 'starving artists' but today, there is so much more of an appreciation, so much more respect afforded the arts that it is almost impossible for us to imagine how difficult it must have been. And yet, they soldiered on, despite the prevailing attitude, or perhaps because of it. There were many art associations, clubs and societies, but they were mainly supported by those who were artists themselves and were, to a certain extent, preaching to the converted. Gladys remarks that there was very little public

Belfast College of Art, 1936. Gladys – in the background, partially obscured – and some of her friends watch as a fellow student paints.

interest in art back then, and while this is true, it is also true that some of the most respected artists of today were working in Northern Ireland at that time.

One of them was Charles Lamb (1893-1964). While she was still in College,

Belfast College of Art, 1936. Gladys is on the right.

Gladys went one day with a fellow student to an exhibition of his paintings in Robinson & Cleaver's. A large department store, it had a small art gallery on one of its floors where artists could hang their work. It was one of the few venues available and as exhibitions were so scarce, Gladys was looking forward to seeing the work on show. When the two girls got there, they began looking at the paintings and soon realised that they were the only two visitors. After a short while, a small man with a beard, who had been sitting at the desk, came over to them.

'Are you interested in pictures?' he asked them quizzically.

'Indeed we are,' came the enthusiastic reply.

'I'll show you around then,' he said with a smile. This was the artist himself, then a man in his forties, and he was only too pleased to take the young visitors around and discuss his work with them. He was primarily a landscape artist and enjoyed painting in the west of Ireland, especially harbour and fishing scenes. Charles Lamb went through every picture with the girls, explaining how he had chosen each subject and describing the motivation behind his work. Gladys recalls how glad he was that here were two young people who were actually interested in his paintings and in what he had to say about them. He didn't know it at the time, but his kind words and infectious enthusiasm would long be remembered, leaving a lasting impression on the young Gladys.

Gladys' friendship with Max grew and soon she brought him home to meet

Art Students' 'Bal Masque'. Committee and guests at a dance organised by the Belfast College of Art in the central hall of the Belfast College of Technology c. 1938. Gladys is seated just left of centre, dressed in white (Northern Whig).

Elizabeth.

'He reminds me of your Daddy,' she told Gladys. This was, no doubt, a definite seal of approval and Gladys was pleased. But what would Max's mother think of her son's choice? By all accounts, Mrs Maccabe was quite a formidable lady and it was only a matter of time before she would want to meet her only son's girlfriend. Sure enough, the day came when Max told Gladys that his mother would like to be introduced to her and they arranged a day that would suit. Gladys was understandably nervous as she reached the Maccabe house at the appointed time, but her feelings were to be unfounded. Mrs Martha Maccabe sat Gladys down on one chair and she sat herself opposite. They had a long chat and got on very well together. Gladys remarks:

'I think she must have approved of me because soon after, I was invited to dinner at the Maccabe's house.'

Martha Maccabe was an ardent Christian

A portrait of Martha Maccabe, Max's mother, painted – at her own request – by Gladys in the early 1960's.

Matthew Maccabe, Max's father.

Max Maccabe, aged eleven.

Scientist. Max's father, Matthew - or Papa Maccabe as he was known - spent his working life in the newspaper business. He was also a gifted poet. Max had one sister, Evelyn, and Gladys became very close to her; in fact they were life-long friends.

Evelyn was blessed with a beautiful voice and appeared in musicals and concerts regularly. At one such concert, Walter Legge of HMV was in attendance when Evelyn sang. He stopped the show, telling the audience he had just heard the best voice in twenty years and that someone should take her on. Evelyn then went to London and received training. Ivor Novello offered her the leading role in Bittersweet, but as she was expecting a child at the time, she was unable to accept. She sang at the London Palladium with the Marx Brothers, and broadcast as soloist with the London Symphony Orchestra. Bill Fairchild wrote a film for her called Song for Tomorrow to launch her into the world of movies. The Rank Organisation made the film and Song for Tomorrow (1948) could have been the start of a long and very promising future for Evelyn Bindon-Ayres, as she became known after her marriage. However, she didn't want to devote her life to her musical career, and chose to spend her time with her family instead. She had two daughters, Diana and Jennifer. Gladys remembers her very fondly and recalls that her own mother, Elizabeth, said once that no matter what Evelyn sang, it touched her deeply.

It wasn't long before Max and Gladys announced their engagement and both their families were delighted with the young couple's news.

Evelyn Maccabe, Max's sister.

SIX

Gladys left the Belfast College of Art in 1938. She had excelled in many areas during her time there and, consequently, was presented with the award for 'Student with the Best All-round Work'. While this was a worthy accolade indeed – and one which any student would be rightly proud to accept - it didn't improve Gladys' chances of earning money from her talent. With so little in the way of appreciation for, or acceptance of the arts, there were almost no areas open to her by way of employment. She did do some fashion drawings for businesses and painted watercolour landscape scenes throughout Northern Ireland, which she sold in some of the art supply shops, but she wasn't satisfied that she was making enough money. Not that Elizabeth ever inferred as much, but Gladys felt a certain responsibility to her. So one day, she asked her mother,
'Would you take me up to see Fred Moore?'
Fred Moore (who later became a member of the board of the Belfast Telegraph) was managing director at the firm of wholesale chemists headed by Sir Thomas McMullan. Gladys' father, George, had been introduced to Sir Thomas McMullan by a mutual friend who had lived in Aberdeen. Sir Thomas had kindly offered George employment in his firm if he was ever well enough to take it up. He got to know Fred Moore very well, the two men becoming great friends. Gladys recalled that she had gone to St Enoch's Church on Lower Antrim Road with her father and Fred Moore on an occasional Sunday morning. She was sure Fred Moore would help her. She needed some experience of the commercial world, needed to learn a bit about business and she explained as much to her mother.
'Are you sure about this Gladys?' Elizabeth asked, perhaps somewhat surprised. 'Do you really think you need some business experience?'
Gladys did not say anything about wanting to earn more money for the two of them, for she was sure that her mother would try to dissuade her and reassure her that they could manage perfectly on what they had.
'Yes I do', she replied. 'When can we go?'

They went to see Fred Moore one evening in his house on Old Cavehill Road. It can't have been lost on Gladys that here she was, looking for a 'proper job' after spending four years at art college. She thought about the stout man reclining on his chaise-lounge, covered with his leopard skin rug, who had tried to talk her out of going to art college in favour of a 'proper job.' Had he been right, after all? Had she wasted her time? Doubts ran through her head, but they didn't linger there for long. She knew that her future lay in art and that she was being guided by a greater hand. Whatever she might do now, it was only temporary – and only out of love for her mother.

Gladys liked Fred Moore and he was only too pleased to be able to help her. Her father had been such a good friend of his and he wanted to do whatever he could for his daughter.
'Of course I'll find you a job, Gladys, if that's what you want,' he told her. ' Tell me now, do you know anything about shorthand and typing?' he asked tentatively.
Gladys looked at him and admitted quietly, 'No, I don't.'
'What about business then, do you know anything about that?' he asked.
Gladys sat up, seizing the opportunity. 'But that's exactly why I want to come and work for your firm – so I can learn about it!'
Fred thought for a moment and then looked at the earnest young girl seated before him.
'I'll tell you what, Gladys', he said. 'If you go to Miss Dunne's Business School for two or three months and then come back to me, I'll give you a job.'

So off she went to Miss Dunne's and really enjoyed learning to type and do shorthand and simple accounting procedures. Fred remained true to his word and Gladys found herself duly employed by Thomas McMullan & Company. What the title of her position was she never really knew, but this is her account of it;
'. . . I was sitting at a large desk with a telephone, entering items in ledgers. Also, I went out to collect accounts on occasions; unpaid accounts. So I had a grand time, walking 'round the town in the morning and going back to my desk in the afternoon.'

On her very first day with the company, Sir Thomas McMullan sent for her. He wanted, he told her, to say a few words about her father.
'Your father was one of my firm friends', he announced. 'I'll never forget him. 'And I'll tell you this', he went on; 'had he lived, not only would he have been a great man in this city, he would have been a great man in this country, because he had the potential.'

Gladys and Max often spent their Saturday and Sunday afternoons strolling along the banks of the river.

Being situated on the mouth of the River Lagan, Belfast had many beautiful walkways. Gladys and Max very often spent their Saturday and Sunday afternoons strolling along the banks of the river, Gladys soaking up the scenic views which she would then file away in her mind for future use in her painting. On one such afternoon, she stopped to let her eyes wander over a particular stretch of the river.

'This would be a really nice place to paint, Max', she announced. 'I could do some watercolours along here,' she said, looking across the water. She suddenly had a thought.

'Why don't you do some painting, too Max? We could paint together then!'

Max looked a bit bemused. 'Well, I was always interested in art at school,' he told her, 'but I haven't done anything since then. I don't know, Gladys. I'm not sure I'd be any good.'

'You won't know unless you try,' she answered. 'Get yourself a box of watercolours and we can come along here and paint together.'

Max took Gladys' advice and very soon, on weekend afternoons or summer evenings, the young couple could often be seen sitting on the river's edge, engrossed in capturing the beauty of their surroundings. Max found that he enjoyed painting very much and his growing enthusiasm, coupled with Gladys' encouragement, resulted in the beginning of his artistic career.

Often accompanying them on their jaunts along the Lagan were two friends – Kathleen Pearson and Marjorie Henry (1900-1974) sister of Olive Henry (1902-1989). Kathleen worked in the same office as Max and was very interested in art – indeed she was an accomplished painter in oils. Marjorie was quite well known as a watercolourist at the time. The four friends would take out their bicycles on a Saturday or Sunday afternoon and go cycling along the riverbank, stopping here and there to capture a scene they fancied in paint or pencil and often meeting artists of the time like Frank Neill along the way. He had, like Gladys' mother, been employed at The Old Bleach

Linen Company before he came to Belfast. He was also on the council of The Royal Ulster Academy for a time. Max and Gladys were often invited for afternoon tea in Kathleen's house and the three of them would enjoy long conversations about art and related subjects. Kathleen married a young man – Ivor Crozier - who had been at the College of Art while Gladys was there.

In late summer of 1939, Gladys and Max decided to go on a camping holiday to the coastal area of Cushendun in Co.Antrim. They were young, with not a care in the world and, even though there had been rumours of an imminent war in Europe, it seemed so far away that it might as well have been on the moon. Although by then they were engaged to be married, it would not have been considered appropriate for a young couple to head off on their own – unsupervised, so to speak – for a holiday together. So, it was arranged that both mothers would accompany the young couple on their break.

They loaded up their camping gear and headed off in Max's car, driving along the spectacular coastline towards Cushendun. Once there, they pitched their tents – one for the ladies and one for Max – in a field overlooking the sea and went for a long walk. After eating, they found themselves tired out from the day and they happily bedded down for the night. The ladies talked among

Elizabeth took this picture of Gladys with Max and his mother, Martha, while they holidayed in Cushendun in 1939.

Martha, Elizabeth and Gladys, Cushendun, September 1939.

themselves and Gladys listened as the two mothers chatted, exchanging experiences from their younger days.

After they had been talking for a while, they heard the greatest rattle of thunder over the headland and rain began to pour down on them. It came in absolute torrents and 'we were practically washed away' Gladys remembers. They found themselves soaked, in the middle of a field with nowhere to shelter. Max took refuge in the car for a while but it was too small for all of them to try to sleep in it and they just had to make do with whatever shelter their tents afforded until morning.

An elderly man came their way next day and learned that they had camped in the field the night before.

'You had a terrible night, then', he said. He told them he was the owner of the field and they were delighted when he offered them the shelter of one of his sheds for the remainder of their holiday. The ladies laid their sleeping bags down there for the next few nights and, despite their simple lodgings, enjoyed themselves immensely. The kind gentleman even invited them all to tea with himself and his wife.

Being out in the open and taking in all the fresh air and beautiful scenery around Cushendun proved to be a welcome break from the city for Gladys, Max and their mothers. But soon it came to an end and, on the last day, they loaded up the car and prepared for the journey back to reality. In their few days away, they had had no opportunity to hear the news- indeed they preferred it that way. Max drove along the winding coast, the car bumping its way down the narrow roads, leaving behind it the long stretches of breathtaking coastline; and the beauty of it all became even more acute when they learned the latest news.

Germany had invaded Poland. War had been declared.

The house Gladys and her mother shared at Willowbank Gardens. One of her uncles sits outside in his car.

Over the next weeks and months, huge changes took place across Europe as the war took hold. People lived under the constant threat of attack and had to become accustomed to their new, less comfortable lives. But in Belfast and around the rest of Northern Ireland, life went on very much as it always had done. There were some adjustments, of course; rationing and shortages of certain foods; the blackout; the restriction of various entertainments; and a huge influx of troops. But, in comparison to the rest of Europe, the Northern Ireland people in general enjoyed a relatively pleasant existence. Gladys remembers:
'Nothing much happened in Belfast for quite a while. Oh, we saw a number of our friends accumulating together with a

regiment they'd joined and marching away down Antrim Road – that sort of thing – and relatives were in the army and so on...... We heard Lord Haw Haw, as he was called, speaking on Germany's behalf and telling us all the successes they had had, of course, in the war; but until then, Belfast had been overlooked by the enemy.'

Until the air raid sirens were heard one night in April of 1941. The people had almost become accustomed to their noise by that stage; sirens had regularly sounded in the city, but each time, they had proved to be a false alarm. However, this particular night, Gladys recalls that although, initially, they 'didn't pay too much attention', her mother decided that they should take refuge under their dining room table once they realised that they could hear 'planes in the distance. And so, the two of them crawled under the table and there they remained for several hours while the raid went on in the distance. 'We weren't too frightened,' Gladys remembers. Jack Anderson, the young man who had been lodging with them at the time, was gentlemanly enough to sit on a chair in the middle of the room, staying with Elizabeth and Gladys all the while they were under the table.

Eventually, the all-clear was sounded and they retired to bed. Venturing outside early next morning, they were very relieved to see that everything in the vicinity of their home was just as it had been. No signs of damage were visible. Regrettably, not everyone had been as fortunate that night. The Luftwaffe had flown up along the coast of Northern Ireland and had bombed the city for over three hours, concentrating their campaign on the docks. The Harland and Wolff shipyard had been very badly hit. Thirteen people were killed and many were seriously injured.

The people of Belfast were totally unprepared for the attack. Although Europe had been at war for eighteen months - and cities across Britain had suffered air raids - there had been a belief among the population of Belfast that they would never be attacked. Air raid shelters were inadequate or non existent and attempts to evacuate women and children from the city had been largely unsuccessful. But they consoled themselves that the raid had concentrated on the dockside, on 'military' targets so to speak, and many of them believed that the possibility of further attack - at least on the civilian population - was slight, and, even in the space of a few days, things started to get back to normal.

For Max and Gladys, there was so much to do; they were getting married!

They had set their wedding day for Thursday May 14 of that year – 1941 – to be held at Fortwilliam Presbyterian Church, which was situated not far from Gladys' home. It was only a month away and, war or no war, Gladys had been busy making preparations. She had chosen her dress and those of her two bridesmaids. The invitations had been printed and sent to all the invited guests. Gladys was twenty-two years old and Max was twenty-three; they were young and in love and looking forward to the happiest day of their lives.

Gladys and Max photographed at the time of their engagement.
(Studio Cecil, Belfast)

SEVEN

Uncle Herbert

It was Easter Tuesday, April 15th, and Jack Anderson had gone to Bangor with friends. However, Gladys' Uncle Herbert – who had first introduced Jack to Elizabeth and Gladys - was staying at Willowbank Gardens for a couple of nights. His wife was Auntie Daisy, and she and their young daughter June, had gone to the family home at Randalstown for a few days. Gladys was fond of Uncle Herbert Mc Cracken. He was a member of the staff of the Northern Bank and had been a friend of Uncle Fred for many years. Through Fred he had met Daisy and, after they married, Uncle Herbert had been sent by the bank to Ballybofey in Co Donegal for a time. They had often had Gladys to stay and they – just like Julia and Willie in Randalstown – took her to dances and parties all around Ballybofey.

Gladys recalls:

'... *They then went to live in Newcastle, Co Down, and I well remember going to see Auntie Daisy in Banbridge when June, their only child, was born. I was then about sixteen, and delighted to see my new cousin – so much so, that I gave her a welcome kiss. In my enthusiasm, however, I put my nose in her eye, which immediately began to water – not a pleasant sight for her fond mother who was sitting up in bed nearby! June, and her husband, Dermot are now grandparents with three children and five grandchildren.*'

Auntie Daisy lived a long and fulfilling life. She died nearing her one-hundredth year. Uncle Fred - who had been so good to Gladys when she was

A portrait of Uncle Fred drawn by Gladys from life in 1936.

a child – married a Newcastle girl – Auntie May – and they often invited Gladys and her mother to stay with them and their son, Derick and daughter, Sylvia at their home.

Well, back to that night in 1941. After they had had supper, Gladys, her mother and her Uncle Herbert were enjoying an evening chat when the sirens began to sound around about 10.30pm. Only a week had passed since the dockside raid, when the bombs had been dropped quite a distance from Willowbank Gardens; but this time, the planes' droning was very much nearer indeed. The three of them looked at each other, not speaking, as they listened to the ominous hum drawing closer and closer. It wasn't long before they heard the sound of a bomb dropping in the distance. With hardly any time to even contemplate their luck in being so far from the terror, they heard another bomb dropping closer to them. Only moments passed before they were deafened by a violent explosion closer still.

Elizabeth rose from her chair and spoke calmly to her daughter and brother-in-law.

'I think we'd better take refuge under the stairs,' she announced.

Without uttering a word, Gladys and Uncle Herbert followed Elizabeth. They stood in line behind her as she opened the door of the space beneath the staircase where the three of them would fit. The sound of dropping bombs was all around them as they scrambled in.

Uncle Herbert and Auntie Daisy commissioned Gladys to paint this portrait of their daughter June, who was eighteen years old at the time.

It was dark in their shelter and the three of them crouched together; Uncle Herbert at one end, Elizabeth at the other and Gladys in the middle, leaning on her mother's knees. Although they felt safer under the stairs, the terrifying sound of dropping bombs was still as loud, and getting louder. With nothing to see because of the darkness, their sense of hearing became even more acute and they found themselves waiting, holding their breath in the deep silences that punctuated the relentless series of horrendous explosions outside. And each time, however much they were expecting them, the bombs brought the beating of their hearts ever louder and their fear ever stronger.

Closer and closer the barrage came. Gladys can remember it all too well:
'. . . we could hear a stick of bombs approaching, one further up the road, one nearer to us and then one terrifyingly near. We heard the glass of our vestibule door smashing, we heard all sorts of crashing going on. It was really terrifying.'

A number of hours had passed since they squeezed into their shelter, but this had been the most frightening explosion. Their house had taken a hit at the front and the sound of it had blasted away any notions they might have had about the efficacy of their refuge. They realised, with a sickening dread that a distance of only a few feet was all that had separated them from death. They held on to each other even more tightly, their only comfort being that they actually had someone to hold on to.
The noise was deafening, the explosions coming thick and fast. People must be dying, they thought. It was so relentless and so intense that it simply could not be any other way.
Eventually, when it became so violent, Uncle Herbert whispered spontaneously into the darkness,
'Can nobody say a prayer?'
Without pausing to think, Gladys answered his plea.
'I'll say the ninety-first psalm,' she announced, and she heard her own voice begin to recite it as clearly and calmly as she could;
'He that dwelleth in the secret place of the most high
shall abide under the shadow of the Almighty.
I will say of the Lord; He is my refuge and my fortress.
My God in Him will I trust.
Surely he shall deliver thee from the snare of the fowler
and from the noise and pestilence.
He shall cover thee with His feathers and under His wing shalt thou trust.
His truth shall be thy shield and buckler . . .'

Her mother and her uncle listened to Gladys' voice competing against the roar of destruction that raged outside the house. In fear and faith, they followed her words all the way to the end of the psalm;
'. . . He shall call upon me and I will answer Him;
 I will be with Him in trouble;
 I will deliver Him and honour Him.
With long life will I satisfy Him and show him my salvation.'

Gladys did not realise when she suggested it that she would have the nerve to complete it, or that she might even be alive to finish it; but finish it she did, raising her voice above the crashing of the bombs. And it was only later that she realised the significance of the psalm to the occasion. The Divine guidance that she believes in was responsible for bringing it to her. They all found solace in those words, and, when at last the siren signalling the all-clear sounded, the three of them were more than grateful that they had survived that dreadful night.

Emerging quietly and with trepidation from their hiding place, they found that the doors of their house had been blown in and the windowpanes shattered. They could hear the sounds of people – neighbours – calling to them from outside.
'Mrs Chalmers! Are you all right?' came the shouts of some young men from further up the road. Gladys, her mother and her Uncle Herbert walked out through the blasted door and into their front garden, reassuring those who were asking that they were indeed all right. The three of them made their way down the garden path and opened the gate. The road outside had gone; it had been completely demolished. In its place were mounds of churned-up mud and rubble.
Gladys looked around her;
'. . . the houses nearby were standing, but most of them had broken windows – as we had - and a chemist's shop at the bottom of the road was completely flattened. The footpath could not be seen at all – the road was covered with thick, broken clay.'

The neighbours came tentatively out of their damaged houses to sympathise with each other. Once outside their house, Gladys and her family were told not to go inside again as a landmine had been dropped at their back gate. It had not exploded, but could do so at any time. Immediately across from the Chalmers' house lived a Mrs Herring. She was a very fine musician and well-known in Belfast at the time. She had come to her door and had seen the state of the house across the road.

'Oh Mrs Chalmers, won't you come in here?' she offered. Grateful for the invitation, Elizabeth led the way over the mud towards Mrs Herring's house with Uncle Herbert in her wake. Gladys watched as her mother attempted to negotiate the mounds of earth, and saw that in her haste, she had come out with only house shoes on her feet. She remembers being so annoyed that her poor mother had gone out without her outdoor shoes that she resolved to rectify the situation.

'I'm going to get my mother's shoes,' she announced matter-of-factly and, landmine or no landmine, rushed back up the garden path and into the house, fetched her mother's shoes and emerged triumphant, much to the collective relief of her family! But before they reached Mrs Herring's house, Gladys looked up and saw a familiar figure coming towards them along what once had been the road. It was her future father-in-law, Mr Maccabe. He had come down from his house in Fortwilliam Park to see that Gladys and her mother were all right and, when he reached them, insisted that they come back to his house at once. Thanking Mrs Herring, the three of them began to follow Mr Maccabe slowly up towards Fortwilliam Park. Picking her way across the stones and rubble, Gladys realised that everything had changed. She glanced back at Willowbank Gardens and knew that life as she had known it, would never be the same again.

Uncle Herbert had gone to try to make his way down to the Northern Bank Head Office, and Gladys and her mother stayed with the Maccabes for most of the day before Uncle Willie arrived from Randalstown. He took Gladys and her mother back to his house – Mountnorris - where he now lived with Auntie Julia and Auntie Susie. Both Elizabeth and Gladys had, understandably, been deeply traumatised by the night's events and, like many Belfast residents, realised that they would be far safer out in the country. No one could be sure that the city would not be hit again. Max drove out to Uncle Willie's to see Gladys and was invited to stay, and for a while, Randalstown became his home. He still went in to his job in the city each day, driving back to the country town every evening.

They all soon learned the extent to which Belfast had been devastated during the blitz. Many hundreds of civilians had been killed; men, women and children, the majority of whom lived in the crowded terraced streets of the city (later figures suggest that at least 900 people died that night). Thousands of houses were destroyed – many completely. Twenty thousand people were made homeless. Whole families were wiped out, whole streets demolished. For many, life was forever changed. The city became deserted as people left in droves. Some were fortunate enough to have a place in the country to stay, but many others simply left the city at night – when they perceived it was at its most dangerous - and camped out in the surrounding fields, under hedges, in barns and sheds – anywhere they could lay their heads – returning to Belfast in the morning. Even some whose houses were not badly damaged could not bring themselves to return.*

Gladys and Elizabeth never went back to Willowbank Gardens. The house and surrounding area were too badly damaged. (Gladys did go back one day with Max and his brother-in-law to salvage their possessions and to organise putting their furniture into storage. However she recalls that she neglected to bring with her the large collection of photographs and information on her father's family that had been kept in a cupboard there. Its absence was only noticed years later, after which time the house had long since been sold.)

In her Uncle Willie's home in Randalstown, Gladys enjoyed the same family togetherness and sense of joy that had prevailed at Oakfield when she was a little girl. Although her grandmother, Martha, had died before Gladys had finished at Brookvale, the spirit of her memory lived on. Uncle Willie, Auntie Julia and Auntie Susie made sure that Gladys, Elizabeth and Max enjoyed themselves despite the war and the terrible night of the blitz. Almost every evening, there was music and song in the house. Visitors arrived frequently and many a pleasant night was passed with chatting, singing and playing music. Max played the violin, Gladys the piano, and together they duetted to the delight of their hosts. It was a different age, one where the simpler aspects of life were enjoyed and appreciated.

Max and Uncle Willie sitting above the rockery in Uncle Willie's garden at Randalstown.

Gladys and Auntie Susie had a special rapport. Susie was the eldest of the thirteen Moore children, and, although she had had opportunities to, she never married. Gladys remembers her as:

*Source; 'The Blitz –Belfast in the War Years.' Brian Barton. The Blackstaff Press, 1989 *'a lovely character. She was reserved, kind and thoughtful. I remember her telling me on one occasion; 'When I'm worried or concerned about something, I just go up to the organ and play my troubles away.'*

Years later, Auntie Susie took ill and had to go to hospital for a slight operation. I went to see her on a Sunday and she smiled and was her usual gracious self. We talked for a while in general and she said she was wondering how the choir had done that morning (she had a deputy playing for the Service that day). Then she said,

'I listened to a lovely rendering of 'The Holy City' on the radio this morning . . .'

And she stopped speaking, but kept smiling at me. Quite suddenly, she seemed to muster all her strength, caught my arm and said,

'You'd better go now.'

This was not like her at all, and I sensed that there must be something wrong. So I kissed her a hurried goodbye and quickly found a nurse. My dear Auntie Susie never spoke again. She suffered a massive stroke and died five weeks later. It was obvious she did not want me to witness what she felt was coming on her and this generous action was typical of her character. I shall never forget her gentleness and kindness.'

Gladys' impression of a city street in the aftermath of a Luftwaffe bombing raid.

Gladys and Max on their wedding day – 14 May 1941.

EIGHT

There was no point in looking back after the terrible events of that night in April. The future was beckoning, and while it would be a long time before Belfast would recover, the people knew that promise did not lie in the past. Life went on; happiness was out there – maybe not today or tomorrow – but sometime soon there would be a piece of it for everyone.

For Gladys and Max, however, happiness was only days away. Their wedding was set for May 14th in Belfast, but it was decided that because of the recent events there, the couple would be married in Randalstown instead. Gladys and Elizabeth re-arranged the plans and soon the family were looking forward to a wedding in their home town.

Gladys had been christened in Randalstown Parish Church when she was a tiny baby. The world had been at war then; and now, as she and her fiancé planned to marry in that same church, the world was at war once again. It was a fact that was surely not lost on Elizabeth as she helped her only child prepare to walk down the aisle. She wished so much that George were alive to see how beautiful his little girl looked now that she had become a young lady. Gladys missed her father very much, but Uncle Willie had been so good to her since he died, and she knew that he would do his very best to make sure that the day would be a great success for herself and Max.

Of course, the young engaged-to-be-married couple would have been a great source of comfort to their relatives. Their love for each other and their uncomplicated hopes for the future were symbolic of the fact that life would go on. There would have been great encouragement from everyone around them to proceed with their wedding plans in spite of such troubled times.

Cousin Beatrice was Gladys' bridesmaid, but it was not planned that she be the only one. Her friend, Margaret Strain, was to have been her bridesmaid too, but her dress had been destroyed in the blitz and there hadn't been time to have another one made. She came to the wedding of course, but Beatrice was the sole bridesmaid.

Despite any setbacks, they had a wonderful day. Uncle Willie gave Gladys away at the ceremony and later entertained everyone with his sense of humour and his singing, so the young couple started their married life surrounded by the people who meant so much to them both. They honeymooned in Dublin, travelling down on the train and staying in a hotel - now long gone - on Harcourt Street, near St Stephen's Green. They spent the days sightseeing, visiting the art galleries and places of interest. Gladys recalls that they went to Dublin Zoo and had their photograph taken outside the monkeys' cage! In the evenings, they went to the theatre, enjoying themselves immensely and putting the events in Belfast of the previous few weeks right out of their heads.

They arrived back to Uncle Willie's house in Randalstown, ready to start their life together as husband and wife. Elizabeth was still staying there as well, and much as their relatives would have loved to have had them for as long as they wanted, Gladys and Max felt they should have a place of their own. But houses were extremely scarce at the time. The blitz had destroyed so many and rendered so many others uninhabitable that the demand for homes was great. However, Max's sister, Evelyn, and her husband, had only recently taken a house in Greenisland, and they invited the newly-wed couple to share the house with them. Max and Gladys were delighted with the offer and moved in as soon as they could. Gladys and Evelyn got along famously and during the time she and Max lived with her and her husband they never had a cross word. Many nights were spent around the piano, with Evelyn singing in her beautiful voice and Gladys accompanying her. Elizabeth's cousin, Lily Shaw, also lived along the shore at Greenisland at the time with her husband, George, who was secretary of the Old Bleach Linen Company then. Lily and George held parties at their home and regularly invited both young couples. Gladys looks back with great fondness at this time in their lives. They were young and carefree, just starting out in life and living it to the full.

But the threat of war hung over them and there was talk of conscription being brought in. Gladys, being a young bride, was fearful that Max might be called up, and she remembers constantly asking him not to join up (an action which she now regards as being quite a selfish one). Max, for his part, was determined to do something however, so he joined the Home Guard, serving in it for the duration of the war.

Now at this time, Max's parents Martha and Matthew decided to move from the end of town where the bombing had occurred. So they sold their house

On their honeymoon in Dublin, Max and Gladys stroll down a city street.

in Fortwilliam Park, and bought another opposite to The Ulster Museum on Stranmillis Road. The house was rather big for just the two of them and Gladys suggested to Max that perhaps his parents might allow them to live in the upper part of the house. They spoke to Martha and she was thrilled at the suggestion, especially as she got on so well with Gladys. So they moved in to the top part of the house and enjoyed the years they spent there. Elizabeth had moved also, to University Road – which is just below Stranmillis Road – to a house which is now part of the Open University, so Gladys had both mother-in-law and mother to hand. Max's sister, Evelyn would sometimes take a break from her voice training in London to come over to stay with them. London was regularly being bombed at the time and Martha was naturally concerned, often travelling over to London to be with her daughter.

For Gladys and Max, painting and drawing were still very much on the agenda and they continued their output in spite of the war. Gladys began to develop a distinctive style and also started to exhibit in places around Belfast. In 1942, she showed her work in Robinson & Cleaver's Gallery and the following year at the Civil Defence Art Exhibition at the Belfast Art Gallery. Also exhibiting there was a young Markey Robinson. He had submitted two paintings, which depicted scenes he had witnessed during the blitz. His *Bomb Crater in Eglinton Street* was purchased by the Civil Defence Authority chairman, who then presented it to the Ulster Museum for their permanent collection.

Many other exhibitions followed, and both Gladys and Max began to become regulars on the thriving - but barely existent - Belfast art scene. Max's favoured subjects came to be snow scenes and fish, while Gladys developed her love of crowds, still life studies and theatrical subjects. Both painted in oil as well as watercolour, using whatever suitable surfaces they could come by. The world was still at war and it was not easy to get the materials which were needed by artists to continue their work. But, in spite of the situation, the small community of painters managed to improvise. Gladys can remember the day George Campbell (1917-1979) called to the house and, in breathless excitement, told her about this new type of board he had come across which would be ideal for painting on. It was hardboard, and he was delighted with it, exclaiming that you could even cut it with a knife.

All those painters, who refused to give in to the adversity they found themselves faced with, are those whose names are so familiar to us today. It

Memory of Markey Robinson 1918 – 1999.

was Gerard Dillon (1916-1971) who remarked that Belfast was a great place to paint because 'everybody's agin you. You paint out of defiance.' While this may indeed be true, it would not have been everyone who would have risen to the bait so to speak. It took a certain type of character to turn that hostility to his or her advantage.

As well as Belfast, Gladys began to exhibit in Dublin. With the end of the War in 1945, came a renewed sense of energy. In 1946 and '47, she showed at Victor Waddington Galleries there. In Dublin, she says, the attitude towards art and artists was more convivial and encouraging. There was an atmosphere of acceptance and, indeed, some northern artists who found it increasingly difficult to exhibit and sell their work in Belfast were to find a welcome in Dublin. The Irish Exhibition of Living Art had been founded in 1943 in Dublin by the stalwart Mainie Jellet (1897-1944) and provided those who were painting in a less than traditional style with an outlet in which to display their work. However, that same year, the Council for the Encouragement of Music and the Arts in Northern Ireland (CEMA) was also born. Established under the auspices of the Northern Ireland government, with funding from the Pilgrim Trust and the government themselves, CEMA also became known as a place where talent was encouraged and afforded a degree of appreciation. And so, within a short space of time, artists both north and south of the border were presented with exhibition space that had previously been denied them. It was a start, but it would prove to be a long time before their work would be taken seriously by the majority of the public; and, indeed, several of those artists would not live to see that day.

The Northern Ireland affiliated group of the Artists International Association (AIA) was formed around this time in Belfast. As well as Max and Gladys, other members of the group included artists Sydney Smith (1912-1982), Markey Robinson (1918-1999), John Luke (1906-1975), George Campbell, Arthur Campbell (1909-1994), Kathleen and Roger Bell and Arthur Armstrong (1924-1996). They took premises in Royal Avenue where they held exhibitions, and the Maccabes were invited to have a joint show there. John Hewitt (1907-1987) poet and critic and Keeper of Art at the Belfast Art Gallery (now The Ulster Museum) opened their exhibition and it was very successful for them both – an early indicator of the broad appeal of their work. The AIA in Belfast would prove to be short-lived, however. The then secretary, who, Gladys recalls, was most efficient and central to the success of the association, was called back to his office in London. A prominent member of the Ulster Academy offered to take over the position, but soon changed his mind when faced with the huge amount of work involved and another suitable replacement could not be found. Consequently, the AIA in Belfast disbanded and this was, Gladys says, a considerable loss to art in Northern Ireland.

Gladys had begun to exhibit at the Ulster Academy around this time, at the suggestion of John Hewitt. Their exhibitions were held at the Belfast Art Gallery, the place where she had stood with her father in front of Sir John Lavery's portrait when she was only a child and dreamed of becoming an artist. In 1949, the President of the Ulster Academy (as it was then known, the 'Royal' being adopted in 1950) the sculptor, Morris Harding (1874-1964), invited Gladys to submit to an exhibition of paintings to be considered for the museum's permanent collection, and she entered a piece entitled *The Bus Queue*. The museum duly acquired it for their permanent collection, and thus, her father's prediction that Gladys would one day have a painting hanging in the Belfast Museum and Art Gallery had come true. The museum also purchased one of Max's watercolours, *Aquarium* in 1950. In 1952, Gladys was appointed Vice President of the RUA, a position she held for a number of years, and she is also an Honorary Academician (HRUA). She was proposed as President of the RUA in the 1990s but, because of other commitments, was unable to accept.

In 1946, on December 17th, Gladys gave birth to her first child, Christopher George. By this time, of course, the war was over and, although it would take time before things could get back to a semblance of normality, there was, nevertheless, a feeling of hope and renewal among the people of Northern

The Ulster Academy Arts Ball, 1944. Left to right; Roberta Hewitt, John Hewitt, Gladys, Max, Berry Wilks, Maurice Wilks.

Ireland. Little Christopher's arrival would have symbolised this for Gladys and Max. They were still living with Max's parents in Stranmillis and the proud grandparents were delighted with the addition to their household. Having them so close at hand and, with her mother only down the road, Gladys was very fortunate; although she is at pains to point out that neither mother nor mother-in-law was intrusive. Both grandmothers cherished their little grandson and Gladys knew how important their bond would be with her child, as she had been so fortunate herself to have had such a special relationship with her own grandmother, Martha.

The day that Christopher was christened, Gladys and Max's good friend, Arthur Campbell - brother of George - came to their house to take some photographs. He was an excellent photographer – as well as a painter – and was constantly snapping scenes of everyday life in Belfast and Dublin. The huge archive he left is now in the Northern Ireland Public Records Office. Gladys and Max often visited him on a Sunday afternoon and she remembers him fondly as a most interesting and knowledgeable character.

Gladys had always enjoyed poetry and had often been moved to write some of her own when she witnessed an event or contemplated the beauty of nature. One evening, as she sat by Christopher's cot when he was about one month old, the thoughts she had formed themselves into verse and she wrote the following poem;

'Wishes'.

What was my wish as I dreamed of you
Through days of sunshine and nights of blue,
As I hoped and wondered what way you would be
And how I should dance you upon my knee;
I wished for a baby fair and strong
Who'd chuckle and crow the whole day long.

The morn I first saw you, darling boy,
'Twas clear that here was no earthly joy,
For all I had longed for through the years
I found in your smiles and your little tears,
In your singing voice and laughter gay,
Your eyes so blue and your charming way;
Much, much more than my dream came true,
The breath of Heaven I found in you.

What is my wish for the time yet to be,
When the days are long passed that you danced on my knee,
When your cradle and toys you have all outgrown
And into the world you step alone;
That you may be gentle, thoughtful, kind,
Noble of heart with intelligent mind,
Helpful to all who need your aid,
Unaffected and unafraid.
That you're known as a true man when life's work is done;
These are my wishes for you my dear son.

Max and Gladys made many friends while living in Stranmillis and they enjoyed that time very much. But as Christopher grew, they began to wonder if they didn't need a place of their own with a bit more space for their little boy. He was, Gladys recalls, very active, and the top floor flat didn't really provide him with as much opportunity to run about as a house of their own might. Their minds were made up, however, when the little boy was about three years old. Gladys caught him one day standing on the railing that ran across the top staircase. He was looking right down between the banisters to the hallway below and she thought to herself, 'That's it. We'll have to get a house!'

They began to look around and soon found what they were looking for in Vauxhall Park off Old Stranmillis Road.

Gladys with baby Christopher. 1947.

The arrival of Christopher did nothing to diminish his mother's artistic desires. While he was most certainly loved and cherished, Gladys still made time to continue her painting and never neglected her talent. She continued to show work in exhibitions, as did Max. These included the Royal Scottish Academy in 1948, where she exhibited two paintings; and also that year, and the next, her work was on display – along with that of Max - in the Artists of Fame and Promise exhibitions at the

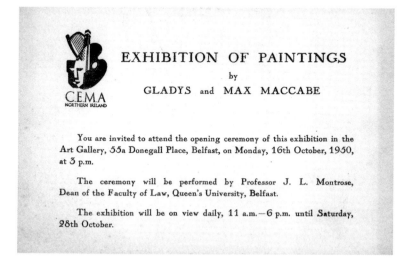

An invitation to Gladys and Max's joint exhibition, CEMA 1950.

Max and Gladys at their joint exhibition in London's Kensington Galleries in 1949. With them are Max's sister, Evelyn, and Bill Fairchild, who wrote the script for Evelyn's film, 'A Song for Tomorrow'. (Photo-Flash, London)

Leicester Galleries in London. In 1949, the Kensington Art Gallery in London held a two-man exhibition of their work, which drew high praise from the critic Wyndham Lewis (1882-1957) in an article he wrote for The Listener:

'Max and Gladys Maccabe share the walls of The Kensington Art Gallery, 15, St Mary Abbotts Terrace. With these very talented young artists, we are reminded again of Ireland (they live in Belfast) and of its awakening visual consciousness. Gladys Maccabe often attains great delicacy. She is anecdotal; the greater severity of Max has a special appeal for me. His fish rival Minton's last month's fish: though they are more tubular, the other's a glittering flat ornament coughed up by the ocean, or like a barbaric tin plaque to hang from a neck-chain. Max's twenty-guinea 'Still Life' is worth at least two hundred. This gallery, under the able direction of Mrs. Marchant, can be depended on for shows of high quality.'

At their joint exhibition in the Dawson Gallery, Dublin. Max and Gladys are pictured with the Countess of Antrim, who opened the exhibition. September 1949. (Evening Mail)

More and more exhibitions followed and Gladys began showing at both the CEMA and the IELA every year. Both organisations were very keen to encourage and support young and talented artists.

Also in 1949, Gladys and Max were invited to have a joint exhibition at the Dawson Gallery in Dublin by the gallery's proprietor, Leo Smith. The exhibition was opened by Angela, Countess of Antrim (1911-1984) - herself a reknowned sculptor and illustrator - and it received extremely high praise and glowing reviews in the press in both in Dublin and Belfast. Gladys has kept them all in her scrapbooks and I have chosen to reproduce one here even though it is fairly long, as I feel it is quite charming and perhaps indicative of the attention this husband and wife artistic team attracted at the time. Artists, per se, were something of a curiosity, but two in one family? Well, that was a rarity! Unfortunately, neither the publication nor the writer is named, but it is obviously from a Dublin newspaper:

'There may have been a time when the Northern painter sort of tip-toed into the Dublin galleries. If there was, I do not remember it; for all I know is the Ulster artist now strides boldly in the Dublin door and takes his place by right of artistic conquest. And right welcome he is too!

The latest painters to arrive from the North are Gladys and Max Maccabe. I met them in Dawson Street yesterday. They were completing the final details of their 'two-man' exhibition, an exciting occasion for both of them for it is their first joint exhibition in the Capital.

It is an interesting show in another way, too, for it is the work of painters who are man and wife. They are a most charming couple. Gladys, blonde, hazel-eyed, is quite the vivacious lady of fashion. She is a native of Randalstown and has been drawing almost since she was able to hold a pencil.

Max, dark-haired, quiet, thoughtful, and slower of speech, is a Belfast man who admits that he only became interested in painting since he got married.

At their first 'two-man' show in Belfast they sold nearly forty paintings, and if you know Belfast as well as I do, that is something of a minor miracle. Three years ago the Northern Ireland affiliated group of the Artists' International Association invited them to hold another exhibition.

Gladys is represented in the CEMA (Northern Ireland) Collection, and pictures by both husband and wife have been put on tour by this body. They exhibited in the recent 'Art in Ulster' show, a sign of how their work is appreciated, and this year Gladys had a picture purchased by the Belfast Art Gallery.

Though this is their first combined show in Dublin, their pictures have been hung at the Living Art Exhibition and at the Exhibition of the Watercolour Society of Ireland, for they both work in oils and watercolour. Gladys has also had a picture purchased by The Haverty Trust. Their most recent success was a two-man show in London which was warmly praised by the distinguished critic, Mr. Wyndham Lewis.

This is quite a record of achievement by two very young artists. A charming pair to meet, they are a warm-hearted, enthusiastic, unaffected team of painters with no artistic side.

Indeed, it is not at all easy to get them to talk about their ideas on painting. They are much more likely to discuss the problems presented by their young son, who seems to be what every young son worth his salt should be – a bit of a handful. But on that point, the evidence is both biased and unreliable: I only heard about him from his parents.'

During their time in Dublin, one of the many artists they saw was Jack B Yeats (1871-1957). He was quite elderly then and Gladys recollects that he would walk slowly around the city centre streets wearing a very long black coat and a wide-brimmed black hat, both of which were set off by a bright red scarf. He visited Max and Gladys' joint show at the Dawson Gallery and Leo Smith told them that Yeats had been very impressed with what he saw, singling out one of Max's fish paintings as one which he particularly liked.

Gladys and Max pictured at the Kensington Art Gallery, London, during their two man exhibition there in 1949. (Times Pictorial)

NINE

The 1950s saw a flowering of Gladys' career. She had found a distinctive style and she was almost constantly working towards an exhibition of one form or another in either Dublin, Belfast or further afield. Her work was chosen to be included in the Exhibition of Contemporary Irish Paintings in North America in 1950. One of her paintings – along with one by Frank McKelvey - was chosen to appear in the exhibition catalogue. A contemporary newspaper report, again unnamed, (at this early stage in her career, Gladys had begun to keep press cuttings, and while she was meticulous in cataloguing them, there are a few that have remained unmarked) bemoaned the fact that the catalogue, while describing the trends in the development of Irish painting, failed to make reference to the Ulster painters included, in spite of the fact that it was two Ulster painters' work which had been chosen to appear in it. The exhibition had been sponsored by the Cultural Relations Committee of the Republic and the writer went on to say:

'It is regrettable that the Northern Ireland Government's inactivity in publicising the Province's artistic life should result in so many of our first-rate artists becoming associated with what is essentially an Eire Government enterprise. There are more forms of propaganda than one!'

The opening of the Royal Ulster Academy's Festival exhibition in May 1951 at the Gallery, 55a Donegall Place, Belfast. From left; JAS Stendall, Director of the Belfast Museum and Art Gallery, Morris Harding, President of the RUA, Gladys Maccabe, Stanley Prosser and Renee Bickerstaff. (Northern Whig)

Other artists exhibiting included Colin Middleton, George Campbell, Daniel O'Neill, Max Maccabe and Rowel Friers. One wonders as to the extent of their regret at being associated with such an enterprise!

Show after show followed and, like her fellow contemporaries, Gladys found that the avenues open to her were increasing. As the artists kept producing, so the appreciation began to grow – albeit it at a slow rate.

Both Gladys and Max became involved with The Gaelic League, which had been founded in 1893 with the intention of reviving the declining Irish language and promoting interest in Irish culture. Their branch met in St Mary's Hall, Bank Street, in Belfast. Heavily involved in it were George Campbell, Gerard Dillon, and Dan O'Neill (1920-1974). Gladys, of course, knew all three artists, exhibiting with them in various group shows.

Many discussions on art were had there with all the artists involved and it proved to be an enjoyable

Memory of George Campbell 1917-1979

and accessible forum for those interested. Gladys also remembers James McIntyre being brought along to the League by George Campbell. A little younger than the others, he was, she says, a quiet young man, genuine and sincere about his painting. He went on to write a memoir of the time he spent on Inishlacken Island in the west with Dillon and Campbell. Entitled *Three Men on an Island* (Blackstaff 1996) it is a memorable account of the summer of 1951, liberally illustrated with work by Dillon and Campbell along with McIntyre's own beautiful drawings.

At The Gaelic League, exhibitions and competitive events were held, and on one occasion, artists were invited to produce a piece representing an Irish activity of some sort. Gladys painted a watercolour of a girl dancing on a stage at a Feis and learned that she was to be given first prize, only to be told later that her painting had been rejected. The artist Padraig Woods (1893-1991) was on the selection committee, as was John Hewitt. Padraig was a good friend of both Max and Gladys; they had been introduced to him by Uncle Willie during a painting holiday in Donegal, shortly after they were married. He had given them both a lot of encouragement and was a most gregarious and popular man.

Years later, when an exhibition of Padraig's was held at the Linen Hall Library, John Hewitt was invited to open it and Gladys was asked to write a forward to the catalogue. At the opening, John reminded Gladys of her rejected watercolour in The Gaelic League.
'Yes, I remember it well,' she told him. 'I painted the wee girl with one arm up over her head like a Scottish dancer, instead of putting both her arms down by her side like an Irish dancer and it was rejected on those grounds!'

Gladys, with James McIntyre, studying a painting by Colin Middleton at the opening of the CEMA Exhibition, Donegall Place, Belfast. (date unknown)

Gerard Dillon was, like Gladys and all the other artists in The Gaelic League, just starting out at the time. He had produced a fine watercolour of a man ordering a drink at a bar. It was a 'typical Dillon' colourful and very distinctive and Gladys admired it very much. So much, that she and Max bought it. A long number of years later, Gerard asked Gladys;

'D'you remember that picture of mine that you bought one time? Well, that was the first painting I ever sold in Northern Ireland,' he told her.

Memory of Gerard Dillon 1916-1971

Remembering it only too well now, Gladys would be pleased if she still had it, but feels Max must have let it go at some point, possibly because he showed it to his mother, who expressed her dislike for the subject matter as she was very much in favour of temperance!

It was in the early fifties that the Maccabe family moved to Mountcharles, on Belfast's University Road. They had found a very large Victorian house and Gladys had fallen in love with it. The time they spent in it is looked back upon with great affection by Gladys. Possibly because it was the home where they spent the most years – over thirty – and also because of the wonderful times she shared there with her family and a great many friends. The house lent itself to entertaining, and this Gladys and Max did very often. Parties and get-togethers were frequent, with the guest-list often made up of the numerous people they had both come to know in the art world. Indeed, Gladys remarks that the Mountcharles area became almost a haven for the arts. John Hewitt and his wife, Roberta, lived in a flat directly opposite the

Maccabes, and the Hewitts regularly had a gathering on a Saturday evening to which they were invited. Many talks about art and literature were had there with the artists and writers present, and James White, who later became Director of the National Gallery of Ireland, was often invited too, contributing greatly to the discussions. Ann Primrose Jury (1907-1995) also lived opposite the Maccabes and she often came over to talk to Gladys about painting. She was very fond of donkeys, producing many studies of them and was an accomplished still life and landscape painter too.

Other neighbours in Mountcharles at that time were the actors Jimmy Ellis - just before he became a national hero as Constable Bert Lynch in the TV series Z-Cars - Colin Blakely; Doreen Hepburn; painter Terry Flanagan; and a very young Wendy Austen - well-known to listeners of BBC Radio's *Good Morning Ulster* Programme.

Memory of John Hewitt 1907-1987

Present once at one of the Maccabe's parties was singer Ruby Murray (1935-1996) She was a young girl at the time and her beautiful voice had begun to attract much interest. Ruby's father was introduced to Max once, and he invited the Maccabes down to their house one evening to meet Ruby. Gladys recalls that there were reporters and photographers there hoping to talk to the newly discovered singer. Gladys was quite taken with Ruby and liked her very much and so, when Ruby's father asked if she would paint a portrait of his daughter, Gladys acceded to his request, even though she did not normally take portrait commissions.

Ruby was performing at the Opera House soon after and Gladys went there to do sketches of her during the intervals. The singer posed for Gladys backstage, sitting in her concert dress, both of them listening to the roar of applause for Ruby's performance. The finished portrait was almost life-size and Gladys exhibited it at the Ulster Academy that year and she remembers that it was kindly remarked upon by Fred Allen in The Belfast News Letter.

The Maccabes became friendly with Ruby's parents, sometimes going out for an evening together, and, on one occasion, holding a party with them among the guests in the drawing room of Mountcharles. David Curry, leader of the Irish Rhythms orchestra which dominated the light music scene in Northern Ireland at the time, was there; as was singer Delia Murphy of Spinning Wheel fame who sang a piece from her repertoire. Christopher, being only a little boy at the time, was quite overwhelmed that Ruby Murray was downstairs, and Gladys remembers that he hid in his bed when Ruby went into his room to kiss him goodnight! This all happened before Ruby went to England to concentrate seriously on her career. She subsequently went on to become one of the most popular singers in Britain and Ireland in the 1950's and '60's, and had a string of hits, at one point having five records in the top twenty.

Ruby was performing at the Opera House…and Gladys sketched her during the intervals.

By this time, Christopher was a pupil at Brackenber House School, off Malone Road, but a few years before, when he was only four, he had become the youngest ever exhibitor at the Children's Royal Academy in London (which is the popular name for The Royal Drawing Society's annual exhibition of children's drawing) with his painting of a dog, executed when he was only three. It was at this same exhibition that Gladys herself had won an award while she was at Brookvale Collegiate School. Dr Viola, from the Society, said of Christopher's work,

'The child shows plenty of talent and has a very creative mind. The drawing is delightful and we are very pleased with it.'

The following year, 1952, his painting – which he titled *Swanee Minstral* – also won an award, with The Society reproducing it on a postcard. When, years later, Dr Viola wrote a book on Children's Art, he used *Swanee Minstral* as the cover illustration.

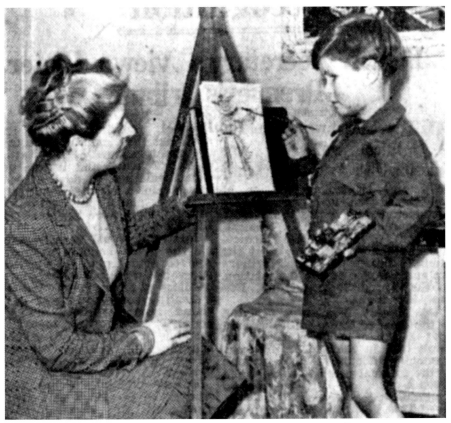

Five-year-old Christopher shows Gladys one of his 'latest pictures', April 1952. (Belfast Telegraph)

The opening of the Royal Ulster Academy's 1956 exhibition on October 17th. Here, Gladys shows the Countess of Antrim (Angela Antrim) one of the paintings she has on display; the portrait she painted of herself with three-month-old Hugh. (Belfast News Letter)

Hugh, aged five, shows his parents one of his paintings.

Christopher drew widespread acclaim at the time, with all of the newspapers in Northern Ireland featuring a piece on the little boy's successes. He also exhibited at the age of five in the National Exhibition of Children's Art in the Royal Institute Galleries, Piccadilly, London.

On 19 June 1956, Gladys and Max's second son, Hugh, was born. Moved again by the beauty of her tiny new baby and of the relationship between art and life, Gladys painted a tender and moving portrait of herself cradling her baby son in her arms. The painting was accepted for exhibition at the Royal Ulster Academy's show in October of that year.

Hugh, like his older brother, had inherited his parents' talent and replicated Christopher's success at The Children's Royal Academy. At five years of age, Hugh insisted that Gladys and Max send seven of his paintings over to London for selection. Thousands were received from all over the world, but only about two hundred were exhibited. Hugh succeeded in having one of his paintings hung and also in having his seven works granted a first class award. Like his brother, Hugh also started his education at Brackenber House School.

A walk in the park for Gladys and baby Hugh, with Topsy, their pet poodle.

Christopher stands to attention for the photographer in front of his portrait – painted by Gladys – at the Royal Ulster Academy in May 1952. (Daily Mail)

TEN

A new force in Ulster art came about in 1957. Latent in Gladys' mind for quite a while had been the idea of bringing together the many women artists who were painting in Northern Ireland. The opportunities available to women artists at the time were not as plentiful as those available to men, and Gladys wanted to do something about the situation. Why should it be, she asked herself, that women are not allowed to become members of the Ulster Arts Club? Are we not as worthy? Do we not have as much talent and dedication as our male counterparts? Surely we deserve as much credit as the next person?

Gladys knew that most right-thinking people would agree with her, but trying to change traditions and rules which have been in place for a very long time is a difficult process and not one which should be undertaken by the faint-hearted. But, never one to shy away from a challenge, Gladys was eager,

The opening of the Ulster Society of Women Artists first exhibition in the Piccolo Gallery, Wellington Street, Belfast, 18th June 1958. From left; Gladys, President of the society; Kathleen Bell; Renee Bickerstaff, Hon. Treasurer; Deborah Brown, and Alice Berger-Hammerschlag, joint Hon Secretaries. (Northern Whig)

if not to change things, then certainly to create a new way of looking at them. Instead of wasting her energies on attempting to change attitudes in places such as the Ulster Arts Club, she set about forming an entirely new group, one which would have the interests of the women painters of Ulster right at its heart.

It was most certainly a case of 'if you can't beat them, join them' for Gladys as she formulated the idea of a society especially for women painters. She called a meeting of her artist friends - held at her home in Mountcharles on December 9th 1957 - at which she proposed the formation of a society specifically for the women painters of Ulster, and suggested that its title should be The Ulster Society of Women Artists. Those in attendance declared themselves to be most enthusiastic and supportive, feeling that the time was right for such a society to be founded. Thus, the Ulster Society of Women Artists (USWA) was born. Gladys proudly stated the reasons behind the society's inception:

'I have always felt that our women artists could hold their own with the men. As well as the better-known women painters there are many others who are talented and would like an opportunity of exhibiting their work. They might feel hesitant about approaching the Royal Ulster Academy, and the Ulster Arts Club limits membership to men, so we are hoping they will join us. That does not mean, however, that membership will be open to every woman artist who applies. Intending members must submit examples of their work for consideration by the Committee.'
Also:
'It is the aim of the society to maintain such a standard that election to membership be considered a mark of distinction and members are expected to seek out and encourage talent.'

Gladys was elected the Society's first President, and her contemporaries Deborah Brown and Alice Berger-Hammerschlag (1917-1969) were joint Honorary Secretaries, with Renee Bickerstaff being Honorary Treasurer. Their first exhibition was meant as a 'tester' show, held at the Piccolo Gallery in Belfast in June 1958. Nonetheless, it received much media interest, resulting in positive reviews and photographs in all the major newspapers. The Society then acquired its own premises in Cathedral Buildings, Donegall Street, Belfast where they could hold meetings and talks – open to the public and to members - as well as life-drawing classes and social functions.

For their first major exhibition – held at the Belfast Museum and Art Gallery,

Invitation to the first annual exhibition of the Ulster Society of Women Artists

Stranmillis, from 8 April to 2 May 1959 - James White was chosen as independent selector. It was felt that having a selector from outside the Province would ensure that the exhibition would have as high a standard as possible. There were now sixty members of the Society. Guest artists exhibiting included sculptor Dame Barbara Hepworth (1903-1975), Anne Redpath (1895-1965), Norah McGuinness (1901-1980), Mary Fedden (b.1915) and May Guinness (1863-1955) As President of the Society, Gladys introduced the Duchess of Abercorn, the organisation's first Patron, who opened the exhibition. Also on the platform at the ceremony were Dame Dehra Parker, Dr Nesca Robb and Mr Wilfrid Seaby, Director of the Museum.

Newspaper reports quoted from Gladys' speech, which included her wishes for the future of the USWA:
'If we can do away with the competitive spirit; if we can allow the other person her point of view, see the good in all styles and generally try to help one another, then I feel we can be a real force in Ulster art.'

Gladys' wish for the society has indeed come true. The standard has steadily risen throughout the years and membership is constantly increasing, even though prospective members must have work passed for four years before becoming full members. In 1960, their annual exhibition was held not in Belfast, but in Dublin.

Artists involved in the Society in the early years were Marjorie Henry (1900-1974), Olive Henry (1902-1989), Mercy Hunter (1910-1989), Gretta Bowen (1880-1981), Kathleen Bell and Violet Mc Adoo (1896-1961) and a number of others unfortunately no longer with us. The USWA is still a functioning and vibrant group, holding an annual exhibition and actively seeking out and encouraging new talent. Honorary members include former President of the Republic of Ireland, Mary Robinson and the current President, Mary McAleese.

The success of the USWA down through almost half a century is in no small part due to Gladys' dedication and flair. At a time when women were very much regarded solely as mothers and homemakers, the development of the society was both an innovative and brave decision. Determined not to be seen as amateurs, Gladys ensured that the society was run along the most professional lines so that its aims and objectives were regarded seriously. Her attitude has ensured that the USWA has done much to further the cause of women artists in Northern Ireland.

One of those involved in the USWA – Mercy Hunter – became a very good friend of both Gladys and Max. They had first met Mercy and her husband, the sculptor George MacCann (1909-1967) at John Hewitt's flat. At the time, Mercy was teaching art at Victoria College Belfast - a post she held for many years. Gladys remembers her own mother recounting seeing Mercy and her 'crocodile of children' passing along University Road on their way to or from the Museum where she often took her pupils for a talk on art. Gladys says Mercy had a wonderful way for imparting knowledge to her pupils and encouraging their interest in art. She was an excellent calligrapher – Hugh had private lessons in calligraphy with Mercy - and also designed costumes for the theatre, including opera and ballet. Her husband George, although chiefly known as a sculptor, was also a fine painter. They were both well-known characters in Belfast at the time, holding parties for their artist friends, which were great occasions and much enjoyed by all.

Anne Crookshank, Keeper of Art, arranging the exhibition of the Ulster Society of Women Artists at the Belfast Museum and Art Gallery, April 1959. (Belfast News Letter)

Gladys with her painting of two children, which was included in the Ulster Society of Women Artists exhibition in Cathedral Buildings, Belfast in December 1959. Part proceeds of the paintings were donated to the World Refugee Year Fund.

December 1959, The Deputy Lord Mayor of Belfast, Cllr Mrs F E Breakie, who opened the USWA exhibtion in Cathedral Buildings, being shown some of the exhibits by Gladys.
(Social and Personal)

Gladys pictured here with Maureen Cashell, at the celebration of the 45th anniversary of the foundation of the Ulster Society of Women Artists in May, 2002

After dark on many an evening in Mountcharles, Gladys and Max would hear a knock at their front door. Standing on the other side of it would often be George MacCann along with his big Afghan hound, Tara. George was a great conversationalist and a larger-than-life character and as he stepped into the house, little Hugh invariably hid behind a door or peeped around a corner to listen to the tales this man would tell, fascinated and somewhat frightened by him both at the same time. He often reminisced about his great friend, the poet, Louis MacNeice.

George died in 1967 and Mercy lived on her own in a flat on Rugby Avenue. She called on Gladys often when she retired and the two of them would have great chats over a glass of sherry. In her early years, before she had ever met Mercy, Gladys had known her brother, Col John Hunter (1893-1951). He was the first Inspector of Art at the Ministry of Education in Northern Ireland, charged with the task of promoting art within schools and encouraging the children to express themselves through that medium. He had visited Brookvale Collegiate School frequently, to have a look at the artwork the children were producing.

Just as Mercy was good with children', Gladys remarks, *'her brother, Col Hunter was equally good. We all loved him. He used to tell us jokes and say amusing things about our work and we actually looked forward to his visits. Well, years later, when*

A photo of Mercy Hunter - then President of the Ulster Society of Women Artists – taken from Art and Personalities, Gladys' column in the Sunday Independent. November 1965.

I began to paint seriously, I met him again. I reminded him that when he visited Brookvale, he used to hold up my work as an example to the class. He was very amused at this. He said to me 'I wouldn't have recognised you again at all, Gladys!' We had long chats whenever I met him. He was a great character.'

Col Hunter's position was a very significant one. The fact that he was retained by the government of the day to actively encourage small children to have an interest in art was forward-thinking and progressive. It may go some way towards explaining the flowering of talent, which became evident in the years that followed.

Mercy eventually moved out to Dungannon, where Gladys and Max visited her. She longed for Belfast and her friends of old, but felt it was too late in her life to move back. She was an excellent cook and on the last occasion they visited her, they had lunch and talked about her days as a school teacher and how she missed all her past pupils. Mercy died in 1989.

ELEVEN

The Maccabes had, by the late 1950s, become well known in Belfast. Their constant activities and exuberance had earned them the genuine admiration and respect of their colleagues and the affection and praise of the art-interested public. Their reputation had grown, and their opinions on art were sought after and valued by, among others, the Governor of Northern Ireland, Lord Wakehurst, and the Prime Minister and his wife, Lord and Lady Brookeborough. It is no wonder then that they were invited by the Young Ulster Society to present a lecture on art to their members. This was to be the start of a long and very enjoyable venture that Gladys and Max embarked upon with much enthusiasm. The success of the first talk they gave led to invitations from other organisations. The word spread, and before long, groups and institutions throughout the length and breadth of Northern Ireland began contacting them, requesting a date for a lecture.

Their relaxed style of delivery proved very popular, and their obvious love for their subject resulted in talks that were enjoyable as well as being most informative.

The Maccabe family, along with Elizabeth, enjoying the sunshine at Portrush in 1958.

They delighted their audience by treating them to an illustrated discourse…

They delighted their audience by treating them to an illustrated discourse which involved them both painting a watercolour to demonstrate their flair and ability, and also entailed Gladys playing pieces on the piano, accompanied by Max on the violin, to highlight what they felt was the connection between certain famous paintings and pieces of classical music. They often brought with them paintings they had completed earlier, so they could show the audience some of their more finished works and explain the processes behind them. Their themes were always, of course, art related, and the views they expressed were very often reported in local and national newspapers. Their ideas and opinions were both thought-provoking and modern and emphasise how the couple were at the forefront of contemporary thinking. The following are a selected few. (Newspapers and dates not supplied, but most from the 1950s)

'If the public do not buy pictures for pleasure, they should remember that it is often found to be good business to invest in works of art, said Ulster artists Max and Gladys Maccabe, in a lecture to Jordanstown Women's Institute.'

'The suggestion that pictures, like cars, refrigerators and other goods should be sold on hire purchase has been made by Ulster artist Max Maccabe. When he and his wife, Gladys addressed a meeting of Belmont and St Mark's Young Wives' Group in Belmont Church Hall, Belfast, last night, Mr Maccabe said, that in spite of an increasing interest in art, artists still found difficulty in selling their works.'

'The importance of the arts in everyday life was stressed by Gladys and Max Maccabe when they addressed members of Belfast Rotary Club in the Grand Central Hotel today. Mrs Maccabe said: 'We believe that a knowledge of art should be part of the everyday life of everybody. It stimulates imagination and evokes new vision, both of which are essential in every walk of life.'

'Art in Northern Ireland could be compared to Hans Anderson's ugly duckling and made to take a back seat,' Gladys Maccabe, the Ulster artist, told Newforge Women's Institute in a lecture last night.
'When will it be generally realised here that, in fact, the 'ugly duckling' is a beautiful swan and should be treated as such?' she asked.'

Gladys and Max.

For a period of over twenty years, Gladys and Max addressed the people of Northern Ireland and brought their knowledge of art to small groups in town halls and villages as well as to such institutions as the Ulster Museum, The Lion's Club, and Queen's University, Belfast, and to Rotary Clubs, Soroptomists Clubs and various Art Associations. They were instrumental in delivering an appreciation of the arts to many who would perhaps not otherwise have had the opportunity to be at the receiving end of such enlightenment. They continued to do it because they enjoyed it, and because they were so passionate about the subject. Payment came in the form of a modest fee to cover expenses, but frequently, if they felt certain groups were deserving of it, they gave their lecture free of charge. Often, recipients of their talks were so pleased, that the Maccabes were invited back to deliver another lecture to their members.

A short extract from some of the notes that Gladys used during those lectures – and which she has kept among her papers - reads thus:

'The age-old question seems to be, 'what is art?' Well, don't we feel it when we stand before a masterpiece, just as we feel it when we hear good music? We are touched. It is most likely that we can't describe our feelings, much less give reasons for them, but there is suddenly some contact with another human soul given by a tune, a picture, a passage of writing or a statue, which speaks to us, often through the centuries. It's a sort of message from one human being to another. We could really describe it as The Revelation of a Human Soul.'

Bringing art to the people; de-mystifying art; making art more accessible and encouraging the public to support their artists; these were always the tenets by which Gladys and Max lived. They loved what they did and genuinely wanted others to appreciate art and experience it as much as possible. In such an age, when art was near the bottom of the list of government policy and political agendas, the Maccabes were champions of their cause. Perhaps they did not realise it at the time, but through the mire of unenlightenment, they helped in creating a path of aesthetic glory upon which the feet of so many may walk today.

Many spirits also traverse that path. Known to us by the works of beauty they left behind, they – in their day – searched wearily for a passage that could lead them to a place where the fruits of their labour would be respected. Only in

Gladys' sketch for the set of a production of 'Many Young Men of Twenty' by John B. Keane at the Lyric Players Theatre in Belfast when it was located at the residence of the founders, Pearse and Mary O'Malley. Gladys and Max were asked to design the set. They also designed the décor for Romeo and Juliet, which was presented in the garden adjoining the theatre in Derryvolgie Avenue, Belfast, in June 1959.

death have they reached their destination. Gladys is fortunate to have arrived at that place in her own lifetime, and many others are managing to receive the appreciation they deserve while they can actually benefit from it it. However, some of those who searched alongside her are lost to us now, but the legacy they left us ensures that they will be with us forever.

One of those was William Conor (1881-1968) and Gladys remembers him with great affection. Conor had a studio quite near to the Maccabe's house in Mountcharles, and she often met him in the afternoons as she walked Hugh home from school. He invariably stopped to have a chat. He had lived near to Max's father's family when they were all young and would stop Max in the street and enquire,
'And how is your father doing?'

Memory of William Conor 1881-1968

Conor had been appointed by the government as an official war artist during the First World War and he resumed this position for the Second World War. He spent time in the United States in the 1920s and returned to Belfast to set up a studio. By all accounts, he was a successful artist, being awarded an OBE and receiving portrait commissions from notable members of Ulster society. However, as is often the case, the outward successes of an artist may not accurately reflect the reality of their existence.

He often called at the Maccabe house and, on one occasion, Gladys remembers him sitting in her dining room, having a conversation.

'You know Gladys,' he told her, 'I never made money out of art. I hardly made a binman's wage. One time, you know, I was asked to send a selection of paintings over to the London office for a small exhibition and I was hopeful that I would sell a few. After the show, a parcel came back to me from London. I opened it up and realised it contained the paintings which were unsold. I took them out and leafed through them one by one, until I had counted out the exact number I had sent over, and there wasn't one of them sold. Not one of them,' he remarked. 'No, I never made anything from art. But,' he continued, 'my sister died not long ago and left me a little money so now I don't need to paint to make a living.'

Conor was President of the RUA for a period, and Gladys recalls meeting him in the street one day in 1957, when he told her he had been proposed for the position. He was, however, undecided about filling it. Gladys urged him to accept and he turned to her with a smile and replied;

'I'll take it if you stand behind me and tell me what to say'!

Respected among his peers and well-known during his life-time, William Conor nonetheless never enjoyed the success he so deserved. As Max remarked once, it is no good for the public simply to admire the work of the artist, they must support him too. Sales of Conor's work now exchange hands for many thousands of pounds or euro and he would surely be most entertained by the current popularity of his work. His surname was originally spelt 'Connor', but he signed his pictures with one n, apparently because he said he could 'never make n's meet!'

An article in The Belfast Telegraph (July 10th, 1981) at the time of the publication of the biography *Conor 1881-1968; The Life and Work of an Ulster Artist* by Judith Wilson, illustrates the dichotomy which was his life;

'. . . he was stuck outside Maze Races one day without any money. He slipped through a fence, ripping a hole in his trousers, and was mentioned in the following day's papers as one of the celebrities in attendance.'

Gladys painted a portrait of William Conor in 1957, while he was President of the Royal Ulster Academy, and she tells an interesting story about the background to it:

Gladys with her portrait of William Conor, which was shown at the Royal Ulster Academy in October, 1957. (Belfast News Letter)

'William Conor's appearance always fascinated me. I have never taken portrait commissions; I have always chosen those whom I would like to paint and have asked them if they would sit for me. One day, I met William Conor on University Road and I said;
'William, I'd like to do a portrait of you,' because he fascinated me. His whole demeanour fascinated me; his little black hat and, of course, his black bowtie. 'Will you sit for me?' I asked him. 'I certainly will!' he replied.
So we arranged a time when he would come for the first sitting. The day he arrived, I heard a knock at the door and opened it and, much to my dismay, when I looked at William, he had bought a new hat.
Now, his little old black hat was part of him – it had a very wavy brim – and this was the thing which had fascinated me. But there, he had gone and bought a new hat with a nice stiff brim and I had no choice but to put this in the portrait. I didn't mention to him the fact that I had been disappointed. I thought, well, I'll have to make a go of it.'

William Conor discusses Gladys' portrait of him with the Lady Mayoress of Belfast, Mrs. Cecil Mc Kee, at the RUA on 16th October 1957. (Northern Whig)

New hat or old, she produced a portrait as fascinating as the man. He sits stoically, a smile creasing the corners of his mouth, his eyes twinkling beneath the shadow of his black hat. There is great movement in the sky behind him, turbulent clouds reflecting the bustling industry of the city below. Behind his broad shoulders, the terraced houses and smoking factory chimneys of his beloved Belfast are rendered with dexterity. He sits majestically above the narrow streets and teeming crowds he strove so truthfully to portray.

The portrait was exhibited at the Royal Hibernian Academy in Dublin and at the Royal Ulster Academy. After his death in 1968, the portrait was put on permanent display in the Conor Room at The Ulster Folk Museum.

Maurice Wilks (1910-1984) was another of Gladys' contemporaries. He and his wife, Berry, lived in the Finaghy area of Belfast and regularly invited Gladys and Max to their house for supper. Sometimes, both Rowel and Ian Friers would be there and Gladys recalls:
'We had many happy times at the Wilks' house in the evening.'

Maurice's preferred subject was the ever-popular landscape. But, nevertheless, he still felt – like so many of his kind – that his work had never been truly appreciated. When Gladys became Art Critic for the Irish Independent, she visited one of Wilks' exhibitions in Anderson & McAuleys's gallery so that she could write it up for the paper.

Alone in the gallery and sitting behind the desk was Maurice, looking decidedly dejected. He looked at Gladys and sighed.

'You know,' he said to her, 'I don't feel that I've got anywhere with my art here.'

Gladys was having none of it. 'Don't be ridiculous, Maurice,' she admonished her friend gently. 'You have made the name of Ulster art in America! You've had paintings made into prints by people like Frost & Reed and have made the Irish countryside known to so many. And, you've done very, very well for Ireland and for Ulster especially.'

'But,' he answered her, 'I feel I haven't done much here. I've been overlooked by so many people.'

Calling to mind this incident today and how sad her friend seemed, Gladys imagines how he would feel were he still alive to see how much his work is appreciated now.

The Lord Mayor of Belfast, Alderman Robin Kinahan, declaring open the Royal Ulster Academy's Exhibition in the Museum and Art Gallery, Stranmillis on 21st October 1959. Gladys is pictured on the left; William Conor and Mrs Kinahan are on the right. A large painting by Gladys is hanging directly behind the Mayor. (Belfast News Letter)

Gladys and Max stepped out of the past and into the picture as Victoria and Albert to win first prize at the Belfast Art's Ball.

Gladys remembers being introduced to Paul Nietsche (1885–1950) at an exhibition of paintings by Alicia Boyle (1908-1997) in Donegall Place Gallery. Gladys and Max were not long married at the time. The then secretary of the CEMA – Jack Louden – was there and called Gladys over to meet Nietsche. She, of course, had heard a lot about the respected artist, but had never, until then, met him. When he heard who she was, he bowed almost to the ground, telling her how delighted he was to meet her because he thought she had so much potential in her work. However, he told her that he felt she would benefit from a little of his expertise and offered to help her with her work. Gladys confesses that she was slightly reticent, and a little in awe, but admits now that perhaps she should have taken him up on his proposal as, she says, *'I'm sure I could have learned a lot from him.'*

Evening life-drawing classes were held by the RUA in rooms at College Square and it was there that the Maccabes first met Raymond Piper, when he was 'a handsome young fellow' according to Gladys. A genial atmosphere and helpful critique were provided by the other artists attending the classes; among them, Stanley Prosser (1887-1959) and Frank Neil. Raymond, of course, has become celebrated for his studies of orchids.

Another notable artist who became known to the Maccabes in his younger years was Basil Blackshaw. Gladys recalls the time when he graduated from the College of Art. An Exhibition of the students' work was taking place in

the foyer of the Ritz Cinema in Belfast and Gladys and Max were invited to adjudicate, along with the then Principal of the College of Art. Gladys remarks;
'We were very impressed that evening by Basil's work. It showed great promise, we felt, and we gave him First Prize.'

Practically all the artists in Belfast at the time frequented William Mol's framing business in Queen Street. A Dutch man, he had come to Ulster many years previously, started the business and, eventually, his son John had joined him. Whenever Gladys went into Mol's, old Mr Mol was always standing with his back to the counter, stirring a pot of glue. John invariably had time for a friendly conversation. Mol's was a great meeting place for many artists of the day.

An annual event for which many of those artists had their paintings framed was the open-air exhibition at the Shambles in Hillsborough, Co. Down. Organised by Patric Stevenson (1909-1983), it was a show in which both Gladys and Max exhibited. They had first met Patric when he lived in Rostrevor and learned that he held these open-air shows every year, hanging

An exhibition of arts and crafts at Mol's Art Gallery, College Square North, Belfast. Gladys and Max are shown here with some of their hand-decorated pottery.

paintings against a long wall near his house. An artist himself – and an accomplished musician – Patric invited them to exhibit, and they both did very well at these summer exhibitions down through the years. His shows always generated great interest from passing motorists and holiday - makers and they were a welcome addition to the Northern Ireland art scene. Patric continued his open-air shows at the Shambles every summer; a good roof over the wall on which the paintings were displayed ensured that the exhibition was never affected by the vagaries of the Irish summer! In the later years of his life, Patric Stevenson was very active in the RUA, became its secretary and wrote a history of the organisation.

Bringing art out of doors was taken further with the development of a summer school of painting that was organised by Kenneth Webb at Cushendun in Co Antrim. First held in 1957, it was known variously as The Cushendun Painting Course and The Glens of Antrim School of Art – and is still in existence under the title adopted in 1961 of The Irish School of Landscape Painting. Gladys and Max were involved with it for its first few

The open-air exhibition at the Shambles in Hillsborough.

John Hewitt, Keeper of Art at Belfast Museum and Art Gallery, opens an exhibition of the work of Patric Stevenson, left, at 55a Donegall Place in 1951. It was the artist's first exhibition in Belfast for fourteen years. Gladys, right, presided at the opening ceremony.

years and it proved to be very successful, attracting students from both Northern Ireland and overseas. Kenneth Webb asked Gladys and Max to be lecturers, and the tutors were Maurice Wilks and Angela Antrim, both of whom were introduced to Webb by the Maccabes. Angela was a dear friend of Gladys; they had met in 1949, when she opened Gladys' and Max's joint exhibition in The Dawson Gallery, Dublin. Finding they had much in common, and Gladys enjoying Angela's wry sense of humour, they hit it off straight away. The Maccabe family visited her at her home in Glenarm Castle and Gladys has special memories of fancy dress birthday parties for Angela's son, Hector Mc Donnell, now known as an outstanding artist himself. Aside from sculpture, Angela Antrim was also an excellent draughtsman and her drawings invariably had a touch of humour in them. She often sketched visitors to her home, but sometimes her subjects were none too pleased with the resulting caricature!

Gladys recalls many days spent out under the skies in all weathers during the weeks of the summer school. Students visited the most picturesque beauty spots in Antrim including Fair Head, Cushendun Bridge and the Dun River. In August of 1958, an exhibition of work by students of that summer's school was held at Robinson & Cleaver's in Belfast under the title Amateur Art in

Ulster. It was opened by Lord Antrim and prizes were awarded to students considered by the tutors and lecturers - Kenneth Webb, Maurice Wilks, Max and Gladys - to have produced the best work, with Max presenting the awards.

The wonderfully warm summer of 1959 saw some twenty people from places as diverse as North America, New Zealand and South Africa gathering in the glens of Antrim to attend the summer school. The students spent a day painting the scenery at Glenarm Castle. An exhibition of the students' work was held again at Robinson & Cleaver's, in March 1960, opened that year by Lady Wakehurst.

Gladys had first met Kenneth Webb when she reviewed an exhibition of his work in the Donegal Place Gallery in Belfast. He was a lecturer in the College of Art at the time and both she and Max found that he had, like themselves, a very strong approach to painting. The Webbs became friendly with the Maccabes and Kenneth asked Gladys if he could paint a portrait of her. She remembers when he and his wife, Joan, came round to their house in Mountcharles and she sat for him. Alas, she is unaware of its whereabouts

Lord Antrim, standing, opening the exhibition of paintings by students of the Cushendun Painting Course in Robinson & Cleaver's, Belfast on 25th August, 1958. Gladys, who presided at the opening ceremony, is pictured sitting with Max; Kenneth Webb is on the extreme left. (Dineen Photographer, Belfast).

Lady Wakehurst opens the exhibition of work by pupils of the Glens of Antrim School of Art in Robinson & Cleaver's, Belfast in 1960. Also pictured, from left; A E Gordon, general manager of Robinson & Cleaver, Kenneth Webb, Gladys and Max.

today, but recalls the many conversations they had while it was being painted.

Another of Gladys' contemporaries was John Luke (1906-1975). While he was painting the mural in Belfast City Hall in 1951, Max would often call by, Luke climbing all the way down from the top of his ladder just to have a chat with him. Gladys remembers him sitting in the Arts Council gallery in Chichester Street whenever she went in to review exhibitions. A pleasant man, tall and quiet-spoken and wearing a long waterproof, he was known to Gladys from her time with the Artists International Association.

The brothers Ian (1909-1975) and Rowel (1920-1998) Friers were very good friends of both Gladys and Max. Ian was an outstanding wood sculptor and Rowel was known chiefly for his caricatures, though he was also a talented painter. Often at meetings of the Ulster Academy, Rowel would quietly execute a few amusing sketches of the members present. He was also a great mimic. Gladys remembers Ian visiting their house on Sunday evenings for

Artists at work during the Cushendun Painting Course.

supper, along with Renee, the girl who eventually became his wife. The young couple were a great favourite with young Christopher and showed him many games and tricks which kept him amused. They became known to the little boy as 'the tricksters' and their visits were eagerly awaited. Gladys recalls the day Ian brought his own baby son up to see Max and herself
'You're responsible for this, you know!' he told her with a laugh. 'I did all my coortin' in your drawing room on a Sunday evening'.
The little boy he proudly showed off that day was Julian Friars, who inherited his father's talent and is a now a celebrated wildlife artist.

Ian Friars wasn't the only artist regularly visiting the Maccabe household who held a fascination for little Christopher. Renee Bickerstaff had become friendly with Max and Gladys over the years. An artist herself, Renee was, as Gladys says, 'a most unusual lady', who was very active in the Belfast art scene at the time. Renee knew everyone there was to know who both exhibited and attended art exhibitions and shows. She was an opinionated person, offering her points of view on both painting and painter, often allowing her thoughts on a particular piece to be coloured by her admiration – or otherwise! – of its creator. But she was a great favourite with Christopher when she came to visit. She brought him little presents and balloons, played tricks on him, hid behind the couch and tossed cushions at him. He very much looked forward to 'Weenee's' company! Renee looked after the exhibitions at the Royal Ulster Academy for a time and was involved in the promotion and sale of the works on show. One of the most esteemed collectors of art in Belfast then was Zoltan Lewinter Frankl. An Austrian, he had come to Northern Ireland after the war and was well known to all the artists; in fact it became quite a coup for an artist to have Mr Frankl purchase one of their paintings.

Gladys and Max arranging paintings by members of the Irish School of Landscape Painting, at the King's Hall, Belfast, April 1961. (Belfast News Letter)

At the Royal Ulster Academy show one year, Gladys entered a very large painting of a Hallowe'en scene. Renee was there, as usual, looking after the administration of the exhibition, when Mr Frankl came in and had a good look around. He was apparently very taken with Gladys' painting and told Renee that he would like to buy it.

Now Renee was evidently of the opinion that paintings on canvas were somehow superior to paintings on panel and, despite the work in question being by her good friend, advised Mr Frankl accordingly, and he decided not to buy it. When Gladys heard the story later, she smiled to herself – and still does at the memory – for she realised that although she lost out on the sale that day, Renee was only being true to herself. It was just her way.

Max with Sylvia Smyth and Renee Bickerstaff, front, in the fancy dress costumes they wore to the Arts Ball, Belfast on one occasion. All three were members of the Arts Ball committee.

Other contemporaries well remembered with fondness by Gladys include Theo Gracey, Rosamund Praeger, Aaron McAfee, Cherith McKinstry, Eileen Ayrton, and Kieran McGoran. There can hardly have been an artist painting in Belfast at the time that Gladys was not acquainted with.

Gladys' career went from strength to strength. The scrapbooks she has kept are full of yellowing newspaper articles outlining the events and notable details of her career. It was Max, she tells me, who first suggested that they should keep scrapbooks, so it is thanks to his idea that we have been left with an invaluable source of reference material. Gladys herself has kept sketchbooks and drawings that go back to her teenage years. Her parents were diligent also in preserving any newspaper reports and photographs in which Gladys featured as a child; these include reviews of piano competitions and concerts in which she took part and also some charming pictures of her among her classmates at Brookvale Collegiate performing in school plays and as part of the school's hockey team.

Looking over the archive she and Max built up is fascinating. Page after page of exhibition reviews – both of their own work, and reviews written by Gladys of her contemporaries' work - reports of exhibition opening nights; features on the lectures and talks that they gave; accounts of any merits and awards they received; Gladys' fashion reports and so on. In all the accompanying photographs, Gladys shines. Always so stylish and beautifully dressed, it is no wonder she was photographed so often. Her interest in style has never waned and her attention to detail is still just as strong.

Gladys pictured at the 1951 Royal Ulster Academy exhibition.

Discussing one of the exhibits, as they arrange paintings for the Royal Ulster Academy's Festival Exhibition in May, 1957, from left; Alice Berger-Hammerschlag, R C Blair, Max and Gladys. (Belfast Telegraph)

Two pages in one of her scrapbooks are filled with newspaper reports from March 1958. At that time, Gladys was elected a Fellow of the Royal Society of Arts (FRSA), with no fewer than nine papers carrying a piece on her achievement. Most of them mention the fact that she was Ireland's first woman artist to be thus honoured and that she was joining the

'... *esteemed company of Sir Laurence Olivier, Sir John Gielgud, Sir Malcolm Sargent and Peter Ustinov.*' *(Northern Whig)*

Another pointed out that, to date, she

'... *is a Fellow of the International Institute of Arts and Letters, a member of The Watercolour Society of Ireland and an Associate of the Royal Ulster Academy of Arts (on whose council she has for some years served.) She is also a past Vice-President of the Royal Ulster Academy.*' *(Sunday Independent)*

In October of the same year, Gladys 'achieved a signal triumph' according to a report in the Belfast Newsletter, when three of her paintings were accepted for exhibition by the Royal Institute of Oil Painters (ROI) in London. She was subsequently elected a Member of the ROI in 1961 and was made an Honorary Member in 1971.

Max had been elected a Fellow of the Royal Society of Arts in 1956.

Max, extreme right, having received a Royal Humane Society Award for his brave rescue attempt in February, 1950.

Naturally, Gladys' personal archive primarily features her artistic achievements, along with those of Max. However, a sobering report pasted into one of her scrapbooks recalls a time when Max attempted to rescue a young boy who had fallen into the River Lagan. It was a February day in 1950 and the river was icy cold, but Max, along with another man who was passing, jumped in fully clothed to search for the boy who had slipped into the deep water while playing with some friends near the first locks. Despite their valiant efforts, they were unable to find him. It was two hours before police managed to locate his body. The man who had dived into the water with Max to try to save the boy got into difficulties himself and Max saved him, for which the man was, naturally, more than grateful. Later that year, both men received Royal Humane Society awards for their rescue attempt, but it was an event which, understandably, was to leave a marked impression on Max for a long time.

Artists Honoured

MRS. GLADYS MACCABE, who recently won the honour of being the only woman artist in Ireland to be elected a Fellow of

GLADYS MACCABE

the Royal Society of Arts, is wife of artist, Max Maccabe, and m..ner of two children.

President of the Ulster Society of Woman Artists, she is also a Fellow of the International Institute of Arts and Letters, among whose members are Sir Laurence Olivier, Sir John Gielgud, Peter Ustinov, and Sir Malcolm Sargent.

Irish News, 8th March, 1958.

In 1965, an exhibition of Gladys' work was held at the New Gallery, Grosvenor Road, Belfast. However, the paintings on display were very unlike those for which she had become best known. This exhibition was a collaboration of sorts between Gladys and the Belfast poet and journalist, Ann Ruthven, (Ruthven was her nom de plume; she was really Ann Young) who was women's editor and theatre critic for the Belfast News Letter. The two women had met some time previously and had learned that they had a connection of sorts; Ann's husband's family – the Youngs – lived in a house called Millmount in Randalstown, farther along the road from Oakfield, and were well known to the Moores.

As a result of reading some words by Ann, which had appeared in one of her newspaper articles, Gladys was moved to paint a picture. On hearing this, Ann was very humbled to be somehow responsible for the inception of a work of art, and it seemed to her that the resulting painting said all that she had wished to convey, and more. Slowly and almost reluctantly, the two friends began 'a new form of conversation'. Ann would put down in words – usually poetry - her reactions to happenings or situations that had moved her, and give them to Gladys . . .

'. . . to ignore or transmute, to change or to enrich as her own perception might guide her. From me she took the highly personal small change of emotion and transformed it in the crucible of her art into something which for me at any rate had the necessary, universal, impersonal quality.' (Ann Ruthven, catalogue notes, 1965)

Gladys was reluctant at first to exhibit the pictures, but was persuaded to by her fellow artist and good friend, Alice Berger-Hammerschlag. Alice ran the New Gallery - which was owned by Mary O'Malley, founder, along with her husband, Pierce, of The Lyric Theatre - and was instrumental in organising the show.

The exhibition was titled *Gladys Maccabe – Abstractions to Writings by Ann Ruthven* and it attracted great interest. The nineteen works included were executed in a variety of media – tempera, oil, glass, cement and collage. In the year prior to the New Gallery show, Gladys exhibited three large semi–abstract works at the Royal Institute of Oil Painters in London, each painting also suggested to her by Ann's writings. This collaboration is one of which Gladys is proud, possibly because the resultant paintings were representative of a deep personal consciousness which heretofore had perhaps not been explored to the full in her work.

Gladys and Ann Ruthven, pictured with one of the paintings featured in the exhibition 'Gladys Maccabe – Abstractions to Writings by Ann Ruthven' which ran at the New Gallery, Belfast, in 1965. (Belfast Telegraph)

Gladys' gouache on board entitled *High Street, Belfast* - which was included in the exhibition - was a response to Ann's poem of the same name;

> Beneath the paving, as I walk
> The unborn, still-born flowers talk
> To my listening feet.
>
> Beneath the tar and roar of street
> A stream entrapped speaks crystal clear
> And I can hear grass murmur.
>
> Rain beats its million heads
> And dies its fruitless death
> On city streets.
>
> Yet as I move, live, and decay
> The rhythm of my being
> Takes from the flowers latent,
> From the spring unsprung,
> From the swift arc of city birds
> A sudden, muted, secret joy.
> *Ann Ruthven*

TWELVE

WHAT YOU WILL WEAR THIS YEAR

Gladys Maccabe, the artist, writer and lecturer, will be in London next week on a special mission for the News Letter.

During an exciting three days, she will be seeing the first showings of spring and summer fashions created by Britain's top designers— among them Angele Delanghe, Norman Hartnell, Lachasse, John Cavanagh, Hardy Amies, and Ronald Paterson.

Her reports and sketches will be appearing exclusively in the News Letter next WEDNESDAY, THURSDAY and FRIDAY.

Make sure that you can share the thrill not only of looking at and reading about "the latest" but, as well, have a pleasant preview of the spring and summer.

Belfast News Letter.

The list of publications to which Gladys has contributed is long and varied. She has probably written millions of words throughout her career in articles ranging from her experiences on holidays with her children, to serious artistic critique. Her journalistic career started in the early 1950s, with contributions to Ireland's Saturday Night; The Belfast Telegraph; The Christian Science Monitor, Boston and local newspapers such as The Larne Times and The Coleraine Chronicle. Some of the pieces were accompanied by her drawings. She also wrote a series of illustrated articles for the art magazine Leisure Painter.

In 1961, she was invited by the editor of The Belfast News Letter to write and illustrate a weekly fashion column. Naturally, Gladys was delighted with this departure and, even though she had her other interests to consider – as well as looking after her family – it was too good an opportunity to turn down.

Fashion was in the process of a radical transformation. It was the era of the ever-rising hemline; the mini-skirt would soon become a fashion sensation. Women's attitudes to the clothes they wore were changing. Fashion had become part of popular culture and was becoming far more accessible and affordable than it had ever been, with sales of clothing and footwear on the increase. Chain stores were opening up everywhere and the young fashion-conscious ladies of Northern Ireland were eager to learn about what was in the shops for them and what they should be wearing that season. Gladys was just the person to inform them. Invitations to fashion shows north and south of the border were sent to her via The News Letter and very soon she was travelling up and down the country reporting on the latest styles. Before long, she was asked to write and illustrate a similar column for the Sunday Independent in Dublin. She was also Northern Art Critic for The Irish Independent and the Sunday Independent.

As part of her work, she travelled to London every six months to review the

Gladys attended the top fashion shows in London and Paris.

Incorporated Society of London Fashion Designers shows, sketching the models as they came out on the catwalk and preparing finished drawings on her return to Belfast. She interviewed some of the top designers of the day, including Norman Hartnell and Mary Quant.

Paris – the capital of fashion, so to speak – was next on her list of places to go. She attended many shows there, also getting the opportunity to speak to some of the top French designers, including Jacques Heim (credited with having been the first to introduce mini-length skirts in his collection) with whom she had a long and interesting conversation.

The reaction she received to her columns from the public was very encouraging and throughout the 1960s, Gladys pursued her journalistic career with enthusiasm. Her easy, personable style was very popular with readers, and it is evident today, reading her column, that she herself very much enjoyed writing it.

A further social diary followed – *Out and About* – in the Sunday News. It was a social page of sorts, featuring items of both local and national interest, covering news about artists, exhibitions, events and fashions. For this, Gladys visited various functions and receptions, speaking with those present and making little sketches of them during the evening. Her photographic memory became very useful in these situations, as she worked up the rough drawings afterwards, and they appeared in the newspaper as acute observations complete with sartorial detail and elegant nuance. Despite the social nature of her column, discretion was quite often called for, and Gladys was occasionally requested not to mention that a particular person was in the company of another particular person; or not to allude to someone's presence at all! And because the diary was accompanied by drawings rather than photographs, she could simply adjust her sketches accordingly.

Gladys had quite an amount of radio experience. She had been both a guest

Gladys sketched the Paris collections for the News Letter, 14th February 1969.

An illustration from Gladys' Sunday News column 'Out and About', 1st December 1968.

and a presenter on various shows for the BBC and Radio Eireann. This, coupled with her experience as a journalist - and, indeed, her flair for conversation – saw her progressing naturally to television.

Her relaxed style and eye for detail led to her being asked to present a fashion slot on BBC NI's evening television news programme. This involved Gladys producing some swift sketches in front of the camera, providing commentary as she went along. She did some similar work for Ulster Television. Also, during 1965 and 1966, she presented an item on *Home for Tea* a magazine style programme broadcast on Radio Telifis Eireann. It was recorded in Dublin, and Gladys was usually given a six or seven minute piece. Her visits to the shows of The Incorporated Society of London Fashion Designers and the latest styles in Paris and Italy provided her with first hand knowledge of the latest collections, which she would describe for the viewers in a few quick strokes, talking to the cameras as she drew.

Here, Gladys illustrates some eveningwear made from Ulster fabrics, 3rd December 1968
(News Letter)

The Maccabe family making music together for their appearance on the BBC television programme, The Nixon Line, in 1967.

In 1969, Gladys' *Out and About* column in The Sunday News was increased to a full page every week, entitled *Fashion, Art, Personalities* and, latterly, *Fashionscene*, incorporating the latest in fashion and art news. Accompanied by drawings and photographs, Gladys filled the page with interesting pieces about designers, fashion boutiques and new fabrics (this was the age of synthetics), always promoting local firms - such as ICI Courtaulds and Du Pont - along with international ones. Also included were pieces on art exhibitions, artists and functions which Gladys attended. Often, when an artist friend died, Gladys would write an appreciation of them for the page.

Times were changing fast. 1969 was the year of the first moon landing. Science fiction had become science fact and all over the world, people were looking to the future and wondering what huge possibilities it would bring. But, closer to home, things were not so hopeful. 1969 was also the year that saw the beginning of what would come to be known as 'The Troubles' in

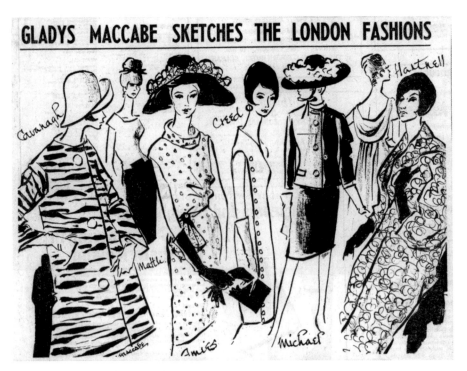

Gladys kept her readers up to date.

Northern Ireland. Fashion and art were far removed from the tragedy of these events, but it is interesting now to see the articles and comment which appeared along with Gladys' page in The Sunday News. On the backs of the pages she has kept which feature her articles can be seen stories of the riots and bombings which were becoming more and more frequent on the streets of Northern Ireland. Like many artists, Gladys was moved to depict the scenes she saw all around her during that time, and in October 1969, four of her paintings were included in the annual exhibition of The Royal Institute of Oil Painters in London. These paintings were entitled *Barricade, Blazing Warehouse, Petrol Bomb Sequel*, and *Funeral of a Victim*.

In 1973, the Imperial War Museum, London, purchased Gladys' *Barricades, Belfast* for their collection.

Protest March

Around this time, Gladys also began writing for the Ulster Tatler, as its art correspondent, reviewing countless exhibitions and commenting on art generally. She still writes for them under the heading *Looking at Art*.

Moving on into the 1970s, Gladys was well and truly established as one of Ulster's best-known artists. Her profile as a journalist, art critic and lecturer ensured that her name was almost synonymous with Ulster art; there was little that happened in the Ulster art scene that Gladys had not taken part in, reviewed, judged or organised. Her enthusiasm and energy were boundless, her conviction unfailing. Christopher and Hugh were now adults themselves, so Gladys found that both she and Max could devote even more of their energies to painting. They both continued to exhibit extensively in Belfast, Dublin and abroad. Gladys had done so much to further the cause of art in Ulster that it was only natural that she – and her fellow artists - should look forward to a time when her labours would begin to bear fruit. It is therefore all the more poignant when we remember that some of those, alongside whom she had struggled, left us in this decade, before enjoying true success. Gerard Dillon was only fifty-five years old when he died in 1971. A prolific painter, his work is now hugely sought after, but he existed at subsistence level for most of his life. His good friend Daniel O'Neill died suddenly in 1974 at the age of fifty-three. He had, only a few years previously – in 1970 - held a major 'comeback' exhibition in the McClelland Galleries in Belfast. It was the first time he had shown work in his native city for eighteen years. Gladys had reviewed the show and noted:

'Daniel O'Neill is a romantic and whether he paints a landscape, a figure composition, an interior or a still-life there is always a hint of the chimeric emanating from the canvas.' (Irish Independent, June 8th 1970)

She recalls the last time she saw him; they were both on the same bus travelling into the city;

'Dan came and sat beside me and was very gracious as usual. 'Are you still painting a lot? How is Max?' he asked - the general pleasantries one would pass on a bus journey. And just a couple of weeks later, I heard that Dan had died suddenly. What a loss. He was a real character and a very fine painter.'

Five years later, George Campbell joined his artist friends. He died in 1979, another great loss to Irish art. His mother, the artist

Memory of Daniel O'Neill 1920-1974

Gladys with Derrick Hawker, Head of the Foundation Course at Belfast College of Art, judging entries in the Rita Rodden art competition for Northern Ireland schoolchildren, organised by the Save the Children Fund. (Belfast Telegraph)

Gretta Bowen, lived to the age of one hundred and one, passing away two years after her son. She had come to painting late in life, often depicting scenes she remembered from her childhood in the late nineteenth century. She lived off University Street with her son Arthur, and Gladys often met her in or around University Road. She was a 'bright little woman' who loved to talk about her painting and her memories.

University Road was, of course home to Gladys' own mother, and it was from there that Elizabeth was taken to hospital for an operation in 1971. She was, by now, an elderly lady and it was forty years since George had died so tragically young. On September 28th, 1971, Elizabeth died and Gladys said goodbye to her beloved mother. Elizabeth Chalmers had been an exceptionally kind and unselfish woman. As far as possible, she had seen to it that her daughter had grown up surrounded by love and happiness, and she had been a wonderful grandmother to Christopher and Hugh. The following comes from a letter received by Christopher after his grandmother's death. It was written by Jack Anderson, the young man who had stayed with Gladys and Elizabeth when they lived at Willowbank Gardens many years before:

Elizabeth Chalmers 1886–1971

'... *then, at your mother's home in Willowbank Gardens, where art and music, discussion, laughter and joy were the experiences of every day. And above all the ever-pervading spirit of homliness, kindliness, good nature and full-of-fun of that lovely lady, your Grandmother, Mrs Elizabeth Chalmers. This is something I can never forget.*'

A string of awards and commendations came Gladys' way during this time. In 1976, her name was included in the world *Who's Who of Women* publication. In 1979, she was nominated an academic of Italy by the Academia Italia delle Arti e del Lavoro. Also that year, she was invited to

Hugh Maccabe, middle, with the mosaic mural - which he and Stephen Wilson, right, were commissioned to design and make for a shopping complex in Frome, Somerset – prior to its removal to England in 1975. Hugh and Stephen were also commissioned to make a similar mural for BBC NI for its new reception area in 1976, and many more for various hotels and similar establishments. Pictured at the back is Pip Thomson who later became Stephen's wife. (Ulster Television)

show her work in Australia and was included in the *International Who's Who in Art and Antiques* and in the *Who's Who in the World*. While these merits were worthy indeed, they all came from outside Northern Ireland and, accepted as they were by Gladys with pride, recognition in one's birthplace, among one's peers, is an accolade that brings the greatest appreciation.

So it was with much pleasure that she learned she was to receive an honorary Master of Arts degree for services to the arts from Queen's University, Belfast. For four decades, Gladys had been to the forefront of the arts in Northern Ireland and now, in her native city, she would accept a tribute, bestowed upon her in grateful recognition of her labours.

Gladys with Max, Christopher and Hugh having received her honorary Master of Arts degree for services to the arts on July 9th, 1980 at Queen's University.

At the ceremony on Wednesday 9 July 1980, Professor Paul Russell-Gebbet, Dean of the Faculty of Arts at The Queen's University, made the presentation speech, from which the following is a short extract;

'Bravura, panache, vivacity, energy are terms that describe much of her painting, but all these traits are controlled by their subjection to the discipline imposed by her training and experience in the media which she employs to convey her own personal vision . . . she is well-remembered in this Province as a broadcaster and lecturer on art, often in two-man shows with her husband. This popularising activity has brought intense pleasure to thousands who have rarely, if ever, visited a gallery, let alone thought about the arts, about their meaning and relationship one to the other – and particularly the relationship of the pictorial to the musical, for Gladys Maccabe also happens to be a talented pianist and Max is no mean fiddler.'

Other recipients at the ceremony that day were Dr. Thomas Whittaker, Chancellor of the National University of Ireland; Professor James C. Beckett, author of many textbooks on Irish history, and co-author of a history of Queen's University; and Professor Denis Arnold, Professor of Music in the

University of Oxford. By coincidence, the previous female recipient of an Honorary Degree from Queen's had been the writer and philosopher, Dame Iris Murdoch, a cousin of Gladys' daughter-in-law, Jenny.

It was a wonderful achievement for Gladys and is rightly remembered as one of the high points in her career.

Memory of Queen's on graduation day.

Just over a year later, Gladys was further honoured when she was awarded the Diploma of Merit of the University of Arts, Parma, Italy in October 1981.

All these awards, in recognition of her accomplishments, came at a time when Gladys was overcoming a period in her life which saw her ceasing to paint completely, not intending to ever take up a brush again. She had come to a point where she felt unable to deal with the idea of transferring her thoughts onto paper or canvas. Inspiration is a fleeting thing, and as such, has sometimes almost fled by the time the artist is able to get it out of their head. At all times, they are turning the spiritual into the material, and putting their most private sentiments on display. To give life to their personal enlightenment and form to their thoughts can feel like a betrayal of sorts, especially when the finished work is then put on exhibition and intended for sale. Gladys says the reason this hiatus came about was because she felt she was 'prostituting a feeling' to commit it to canvas. The pleasure derived from painting a picture was denied her and her career was put on hold. Thankfully however, this time lasted only about three or four years, after which she felt able to get back to painting on a regular basis.

In 1985, two more accolades came Gladys' way. She was awarded the prestigious World Culture Prize by the Committee for World Culture,
'... *in acknowledgement of cultural and professional zeal shown in your field of activity and of your important contribution to the improvement of present-day society.*'

She was also conferred with the title of Cavalier of the Arts by the Accademia Bedriacense in Italy,
'... *in recognition of your contribution to the defence of the fundamental principles of authenticity in contemporary visual art.*'

Recipients of Honorary Degrees at Queen's University, 9th July 1980. From left; Professor James Beckett, Professor Denis Arnold, Gladys Maccabe, Dr. Thomas Whittaker, Chancellor of the National University of Ireland.

THIRTEEN

Towards the end of the 1980s, the proprietors of The George Gallery in Dublin – Derek Shortall and myself, Susan Stairs - made contact with Gladys. We had seen her work regularly at auction and had bought a number of her paintings over the previous few years. Realising that she was an artist with a wealth of talent and a hugely interesting career, we felt the time was right for a retrospective exhibition of her work. Although her paintings were familiar to many, the story of her life, especially to those outside of Ulster, was not. Here was an artist who had been painting since childhood, who had been involved in the art scene in Ireland as both artist and critic and who had been exhibiting with some of the most well-respected Irish artists for five decades and yet, an essential assessment of her work had never been carried out. We proposed that we publish a generous catalogue with plenty of illustrations and explanatory text. Gladys was most enthusiastic about the project, so we began preparing for the show, which would take place in late 1989.

Cover of Gladys' retrospective catalogue, featuring her painting 'Stage Door'.

When the exhibition – entitled *Gladys Maccabe, A Lifetime of Art – The Retrospective* - opened on October 17th, there were eighty-seven pictures on show at the gallery's premises in South Frederick Street, Dublin. I researched and wrote a sixty-four page colour catalogue to accompany the show, which was available at the gallery and also in bookshops in Dublin and Belfast. Paintings and drawings from the 1940s, '50s, '60s, '70s and '80s were featured. Crowd scenes, still-life studies and horse studies predominated, but also included were

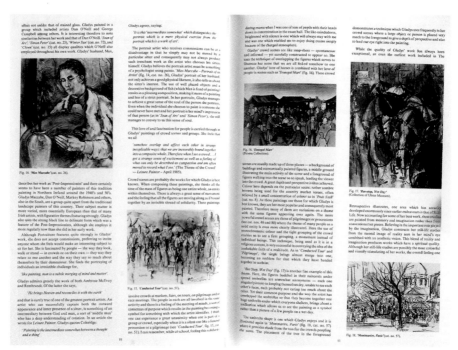

Some pages from 'Gladys Maccabe, A Lifetime of Art – The Retrospective'

sketches and watercolours of places Gladys had seen on trips abroad and around Ireland. Every painting was illustrated in the catalogue; explanatory text and descriptive notes were included, as were detailed commentaries on both the artist's life and work.

The Retrospective was an unequivocal success. Gladys and Max travelled down to Dublin for the opening night to witness the great attendance and huge interest. Over seventy paintings were sold before the exhibition closed on November 17th – a tremendous achievement for a living artist. Attracting media interest both in the north and the south of the country, the Retrospective ensured that Gladys' name and work was once more to the forefront of the Irish art scene. Evident from the number of buyers and interested viewers was the amount of younger collectors who were introduced to her work by the Retrospective. Regard – and demand - for her work increased significantly, as did, accordingly, the prices achieved for her paintings at both auctions and subsequent exhibitions.

In 1988, we had mounted a major Retrospective of the work of Markey Robinson which had also been an enormous success. We felt an affinity with the period both Markey and Gladys had been associated with and looked around at the other artists who had been painting in Belfast during the 1940s and beyond. There were so many - most of whom I have mentioned already in these pages - who had painted and exhibited together, and yet, no critical treatise on their collective work had been produced. They had much in common, these artists. Allied to the fact that they all lived and painted in Belfast, was the certainty that there were definite comparable influences in their work. It was an interesting concept, and one which we felt required further exploration. Some of the artists had, by then, passed away, their existence known to many only from the legacy they left in the form of their paintings. Scant mention of them in the few books on Irish art in existence was all the honour afforded them up to that point.

Perhaps because these artists had not officially bound themselves into a group while they were active, they had not been seen as belonging to a specific genre. (And, of course, it is hindsight which usually affords us the wherewithal to recognise a common purpose.) But close inspection revealed that they did indeed belong together. So much about them was similar. Figurative works featured strongly in their paintings, and, just as there had

Gladys, right, with Susan Stairs, middle, and Madge Campbell, left - wife of the late George Campbell - at the Opening Night of 'The Irish Figurists and Figurative Painting in Irish Art' at the George Gallery, Lower Baggot Street, Dublin, 13th November 1990.

Cover of 'The Irish Figurists and Figurative Painting in Irish Art' published 1990, featuring Woman in White by Markey Robinson.

been a definite – and recognised - group of Ulster landscape painters, there had been, as we now discovered, a definite group of figurative painters as well. We felt that a critical appraisal of these artists was long overdue and wanted to place them within the wider context of Irish art, to give them, so to speak, the status which was so rightfully theirs. We planned a major exhibition, accompanied by a significant publication.

We chose a core group of artists around which to centre our work, and Gladys was one of them. The others were her contemporaries Markey Robinson, George Campbell, Daniel O'Neill and Gerard Dillon. A year of work culminated in the exhibition entitled *The Irish Figurists and Figurative Painting in Irish Art* opening in The George Gallery's new premises in Baggot Street, Dublin on November 13th 1990. Over 120 paintings were hanging, the majority for sale, but a select few on loan. The works of the five featured artists made up for approximately eighty of the paintings, the rest being by various figurative painters both past and contemporary. A three-hundred page colour illustrated catalogue of the same name, which I had written over the course of the year, was published to accompany the exhibition. The catalogue was extremely well received and reviewed. It was sold in bookshops throughout the country – north and south, and in Britain. Within its text, I attempted to explain the reasoning behind the inception of the exhibition. Being aware that we were coining a new collective term and, by this process, seeking to strengthen the importance of the artists within the history of Irish art, it was essential that we provide as much back up for our theory as we could. A comparative study

Especially for the reprint of 'The Irish Figurists' in 1999, Gladys painted portraits of the five featured artists, which were reproduced both inside the book and on the back cover. Clockwise from top left: Gerard Dillon, George Campbell, Dan O'Neill, Markey Robinson and, in the centre, Gladys Maccabe.

of the lives and work of the five featured artists outlined their strong common influences as well as the similarity of their approach. Illustrations showed that there could be no doubt they had a shared early style, and factual evidence demonstrated that their links to each other were both firm and deep-rooted. It was an ambitious project, and one of which I am proud; however, it is one which would not have been possible without Gladys. It was she who provided the springboard from which we jumped. Having worked with her on her retrospective and consequently learning so much about the period from her, we were catapulted into action, determined to give Gladys and her contemporaries a greater amount of recognition than they had hitherto been afforded.

There were fifteen paintings by Gladys in the show. Works from each decade from the '40s to the '90s featured, including the portrait *George Campbell as a Gypsy*, a small but evocative depiction of the artist as Gladys remembered him, at a fancy dress party in the late 1940s. The full range of her repertoire was represented, including horse fairs, race days, portraits, landscapes and a particularly stunning still life painted especially for the exhibition. Further notes on Gladys' life and work were highlighted, along with photographs from her own collection.

The book was reprinted in 1999, under the title *The Irish Figurists*, in hardback, with some alterations. Limited to 1000 copies, each numbered and signed, the first fifty came in a boxed set complete with an original sketch by Gladys. Featured on the back cover were portraits - commissioned from Gladys especially for the reprint - of the five featured artists. Sadly, early 1999 had seen the death of Markey Robinson, leaving Gladys the only one of the five artists still with us.

In the 1980s, Gladys and Max had moved from Mountcharles. The big house was hard to heat in the wintertime and had seemed to become even bigger since both Christopher and Hugh had moved out. Christopher had married Jenny Livingston, the daughter of the distinguished Belfast surgeon, and was employed in the higher reaches of the Civil Service, and Hugh was a graphic artist with BBC NI. There had been many happy times for the Maccabe family in Mountcharles; almost thirty years of memories. It was the house that had seen many of Ulster's finest artists wander through its rooms. Its walls rang with the sounds of laughter and storytelling, and music had drifted out of its windows on many a night. The whole area had become synonymous with the arts, and many of those involved in the art and entertainment world lived there. So it was with great reluctance that they closed the door behind them for the last time and moved to a more manageable house in south Belfast.

But Gladys is now without her beloved Max. He passed away in early 2000 after a short illness. Fifty-nine years of married life had been given to them and their friendship stretched as far back as their childhood. Now, Gladys had lost her husband and dearest friend. Theirs had been the truest of partnerships; they had accompanied one another not only as husband and wife, but in their work as musicians and artists as well. Gladys and Max inspired each other; he took up painting at her suggestion; she continued hers with his encouragement. Together, they made the world around them a richer and more enjoyable place. They saw beauty in their surroundings, capturing it with pencil and paint, making sketches and paintings wherever they travelled. Time was always made for their art, no matter how long the day or how many the commitments and they never tired of it.

A radio interview the couple gave in 1954 to the BBC's Women's Hour *In Partnership* series

Max enjoying his role as grandfather.

Max and Gladys, playing with their grandchildren

illustrates how deeply they felt about their shared passion, and also, how much they enjoyed each other's company. The interviewer asked if they thought it a good idea to talk about their work at home. Max replied first;

'Well, whether good or not, we certainly do so and our discussions range from the best way to apply the paint to what we will next exhibit. Of course, should we be preparing for an exhibition of our work, we have to work the details out at home. So much so that our small son, Christopher sometimes has to bring us back to work with something (like) 'Are you talking about painting again?'

Gladys then answered;

'As Max says, if we happen to be arranging for an exhibition or perhaps discussing the title for a lecture we may be giving on art, we often talk up until the small hours of the morning and only realise when we stop that the fire has gone out and that we're frozen stiff, but we haven't even noticed before because we've been so interested in our discussion!'

How fortunate they were to have a shared interest, one that allowed them to converse with each other, seek each other's opinion and ask one another's advice. The image of the two of them, warmed by the passionate interest they both had in the ideas of the other, basking in the glow of their conversation while sitting before the deadened grate - cold only reaching them when their conversation finished - is the one which I like to think is most apt in illustrating their relationship.

Max and Gladys acted as adjudicators for the Antrim and District Road Safety Poster Competition for many years. Here, they are pictured with secretary R L Peacocke in 1989.

Living without the man she had shared her life with for almost sixty years was never going to be easy for Gladys. For many, there would have been little to enjoy after the death of a lifelong partner, but Gladys finds solace in her painting. Even while Max was ill, it was her paints she turned to in the evenings on her return from visiting him in hospital. In her studio, away from the sadness she was going through, she could find the serenity and company she longed for. In the darkest hours, it was the talent she was blessed with which guided her through. Without it, she was lost. Max was such a personality, always looking for the humour in a situation, never losing the opportunity to make a wry remark or a good-natured gibe, that the loss of his presence was all the more acute. Painting has eased that loss somewhat for Gladys and she finds herself today busier than ever. She works almost every day, at least when time allows, still – curiously – painting with her left hand, yet signing and writing with her right. She continues to write for Ulster Tatler and is still much involved with The Ulster Society of Women Artists.

Together at one of Gladys' exhibitions.

Max Maccabe 1917–2000

It is no wonder then, after more than sixty years spent promoting the arts in Ulster, that Gladys received the honour of being appointed a Member of the Order of the British Empire (MBE) for services to the arts by Her Majesty Queen Elizabeth on November 21st 2000. It was a terrific achievement and richly deserved. Twenty years had passed since Gladys had been awarded an Honorary MA by Queen's University and here she was, still tirelessly working to promote appreciation and understanding of the arts.

The presentation ceremony was to be held at Buckingham Palace and Gladys, naturally, was looking forward to it immensely. As it was such an important occasion, her family suggested she buy herself a new hat to compliment whatever she chose to wear. Well, she looked around at many hats, but could find none that would suit. Most were large-brimmed and she says she thought to herself; *'I'm not very tall, and if I wear one of those I'll look like a mushroom!'* So off she went home and decided not to worry too much about it; something would turn up she told herself.

Gladys was appointed a Member of the Order of the British Empire (MBE) for services to the arts by Her Majesty Queen Elizabeth II on 21 November 2000. (BCA Films)

Gladys is pictured here with, from left, her daughter-in-law, Jenny, and sons Christopher and Hugh, having received her MBE (Ulster Tatler)

And so it did. One day, while looking through her wardrobe, she came across something she had almost forgotten about hidden away on the top shelf. Taking it down, she realised it was a red crocheted hat which her late mother had made for her forty years before. It was perfect:
'This is the hat I'm going to wear to the palace!'
So it came to be, there in Buckingham Palace, that Gladys felt the presence of her dear mother with her. However, being without Max tinged the occasion with sadness, for he would have loved to have seen Gladys so honoured. But with her on the day were Hugh and Christopher, and Christopher's wife, Jenny.
'Her Majesty is really very easy to talk to', Gladys told me. *'She greeted me with a handshake of course, and said 'You're a painter?' So I said 'Yes' and we had quite a little chat. But we were told beforehand that when she put out her hand to shake it, that was your signal to go! But she was very easy, very nice and I enjoyed talking to her. You could talk to her at any time – that's how I felt anyway.'*

Oakfield, Randalstown, in recent times.

A long road had been travelled from the country lanes around Randalstown to the gracious rooms of Buckingham Palace. To the little girl who stood with her father in front of Sir John Lavery's portrait all of seventy years before and dreamed of becoming an artist, this latest honour was a triumph indeed.

There are few alive today who were once part of her circle, few who are left who can relate the story of their life and the path they took. Fewer indeed who have achieved so much along the way and given so much of their time and talent to enrich the lives of others.

Gladys would be the first to acknowledge the debt she owes to her parents, for it was their encouragement and their belief in their daughter's talent that was instrumental in helping her achieve so much. Without their interest, it is possible that her talent might not have been recognised and nurtured to the extent that it was. Attending Brookvale Collegiate School, which actively encouraged participation in the arts, also did much to further strengthen Gladys' ambition. The resolve she showed in overcoming any negativity she encountered later on is indicative of the determination with which she was blessed; a determination which is founded upon a simple desire; the desire to paint.

Gladys' grandchildren, Jayne, Rebecca and Simon.
(Gerry Coe, 2003)

Gladys with her Auntie Daisy, who lived until shortly before her one-hundredth birthday.

Behind the mountain of work that she has done over the years – organising, lecturing, writing, encouraging - there has been the guiding inspiration of her talent. To that gift she has always remained true, despite the times when it might have been easier to simply tell herself she hadn't the time for painting. As a young mother, for instance, when time to oneself is precious and scant, she never allowed herself to neglect her talent; she always found time for it. Even now, the motivation is still there; ceasing to paint would be unthinkable to her. Along with that, has been the fundamental conviction that whatever life throws at her, she will be guided by a divine hand. Professing herself not to be a strongly religious person, Gladys is nonetheless faithful in her belief that throughout her life she has been pointed along a certain path by a force that has had her very best interests at heart. Even when events took a particular turn and things seemed not to be going the way she would have liked them to, she has been able to look back with a wisdom that tells her that their occurrence was for a reason. Each happening, no matter how difficult at the time, she now sees as being a paving stone forming the path upon which she has travelled.

Gladys' cousin, Dr Margaret Moore. An educational psychologist, she lectured at Queen's University and Ulster Polytechnic. She also had several books published by Collins.

It is without doubt that Gladys, along with Max, did much to show the people of Ulster how important art is to us all. Their lectures, given throughout the length and breadth of Northern Ireland brought an appreciation of art and music to the public, some of whom might not otherwise have been given the opportunity. Art and music cross boundaries and divides; no specific criteria are required for their appreciation, no religious denomination or allegiance to specific 'sides' are a requirement for the enjoyment of the arts. Through music and art, people gather together to admire, enjoy and participate. Fostering an interest in the arts has always been at the heart of Gladys' involvement. Her eagerness to bring about a greater awareness among the public is demonstrated by a dislike of anything that might be seen as too elitist or cliquish. Her whole approach to her art - in both technique and subject matter – reflects this attitude; her paintings are instantly appealing, depicting ordinary people going about their daily lives. There is nothing confusing or complex about her work, rather, there is a certain pure and unpretentious quality that allows for broad appeal. There, in her paintings, we can see ourselves, our neighbours, our friends. She makes a connection with us, and that, I believe, is probably the most important thing an artist can do.

Gladys is a true lady – and indeed during the course of writing this book and having written her name so many times – I was struck that the middle four letters of her name spell out that very word. She is gracious and kind and very generous with her time, and as full of verve as one less than half her age. Her three grandchildren are very fortunate to have her love and support – as are all the members of her family, and, indeed her friends. Gladys is enormously elegant and has not allowed the progression of the years to diminish, in any way, her interest in style and fashion. While she acknowledges that she rarely buys clothes any more, the very fact that she can wear items that have been in her wardrobe for years and still appear so up to date, chic and young, is testament to her taste and flair.

Her work has gained hugely in popularity in recent years as art buyers have begun to appreciate her significance in relation to the development of Irish art and at this stage in her life, she is richly deserving of any rewards that come her way. She has worked tirelessly to promote the arts for a very long time, with never a thought for self-gain.

In the BBC radio interview that she and Max gave in 1954, Max was asked to describe his partner in just one word. Unable to do justice to his wife with merely one, he instead used five, announcing that Gladys was, to him,
a pearl of great price.
What a beautiful description, and how very right he was.

Gladys and Max Maccabe.

PAINTINGS

A representative selection of Gladys' paintings is reproduced over the following pages. Nearly all her work is, as the title of this book suggests, drawn from memory, and although, over the years, Gladys' style may have evolved from a darker, more heavily impastoed approach in earlier years, to a lighter, more deft method today, her subject matter - and obvious love of it - remains. Indeed, any variation in approach is as much to do with changing her chosen medium from that of oils to acrylics, as it is to do with the evolution of style. She favours acrylics because of their free-flowing properties, and generally uses board instead of canvas, as she prefers a smoother surface.

While she enjoys painting some landscapes and still life studies, it is her figurative work for which she is best known. If she relies on her memories for inspiration, then we can assume that she was at her happiest when surrounded by people. She has spoken of her belief that we are all *'inexorably bound together'* and it is this conviction that has most influenced her choice of subject matter. Perhaps being an only child, but at the same time being part of a large extended family, Gladys learned the value of belonging very early on in her life. As a child, her inquisitive and personable nature ensured that she forged connections with people wherever she went. It is evident from her work that she enjoys being in the middle of the throng, and likes to observe multitudes of people with a common purpose. Whether Gladys depicts them at a market, a dance, a fair, an auction, or simply strolling in the park, she manages to translate to us a definite sense of unity and harmony.

The paintings included here are intended to give a flavour of Gladys' work. While some are earlier works, most are relatively recent, and, as such, enable us to see how, after almost seventy years of painting, Gladys Maccabe is still 'drawing from memory'.

Gladys Maccabe's work is in the permanent collections of:

The Royal Ulster Academy
The Ulster Museum
The Arts Council of Northern Ireland
The Queen's University, Belfast
The Imperial War Museum, London
The Arts Council of Ireland
The Irish National Self Portrait Collection
Longford County Library
The Thomas Haverty Trust

Gladys' painting *The Library* will be reproduced on the jacket of the *Cambridge Guide to Literature in English* (2005) published by Cambridge University Press.

Facing Page: *My Grandmother, Martha.*

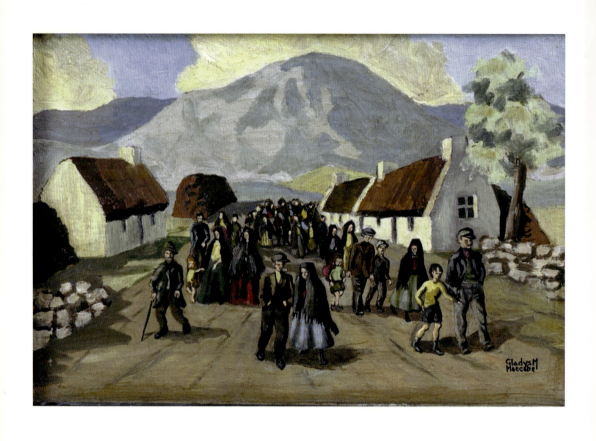

Sunday Morning, Village in the West

The Sweet Shop

The Evening Dance

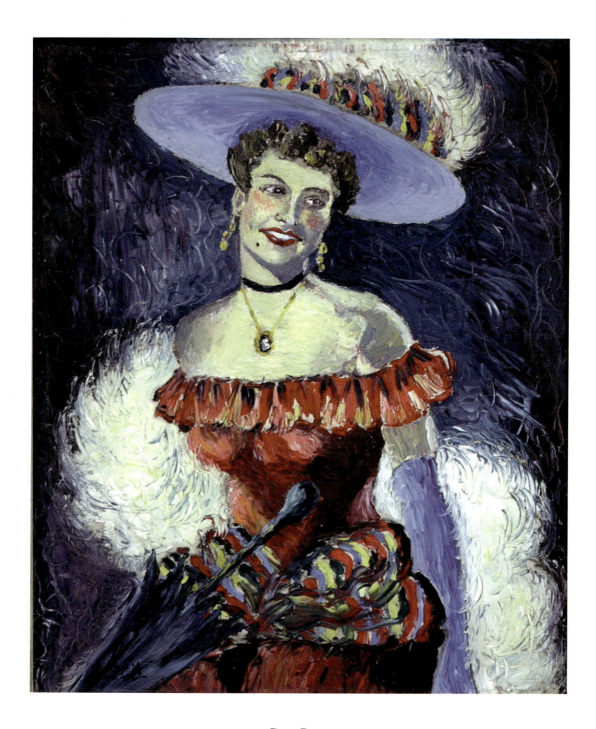

Dress Dance

Going to Mass

Busy Irish Village

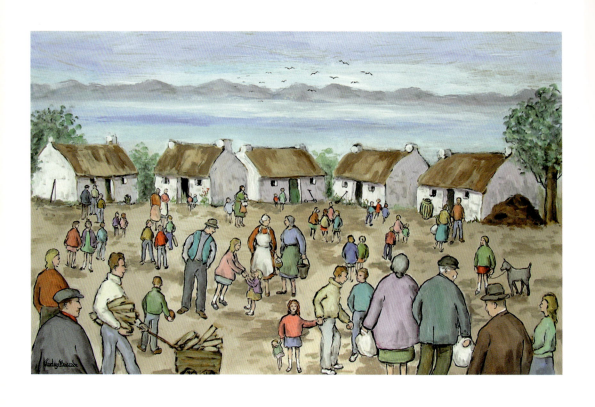

Saturday Morning in Kerry

Paris Street Scene

Bubbling Clown

Ladies Day

Belfast Street Scene

Killarney Village

The Red Hat

Studio Still Life

Village Market Day

EXHIBITIONS

1942	Robinson & Cleaver's Gallery, Belfast	1958,'59	Royal Scottish Academy (Group show)
1943	Civil Defence Art Exhibition, Belfast Art Gallery (Group show)	1958-2004	Ulster Society of Women Artists, Belfast, Dublin, U.K. each year
1944,'45	Artists International Association, Belfast (Group and two-man shows)	1959	The Cobbles, Belfast
1945-2004	Royal Institute of Oil Painters, London (Group shows, each year)	1960	Royal Hibernian Academy. Dublin
		1960	Ulster Arts Club, Belfast Art Gallery (Group show)
1946	Victor Waddington Galleries, Dublin	1960	Womens Institute Club, Belfast
1946	Cottar's Kitchen Gallery, Belfast	1960	Glens of Antrim School of Art Exhibition, Robinson & Cleaver's, Belfast
1947	Victor Waddington Galleries, Dublin		
1947	Leger Galleries, London	1961	Ritchie Hendriks Gallery, Dublin (Two-man show with Max Maccabe)
1948	National Gallery of Canada, Ottawa		
1948	Royal Scottish Academy (Group show)	1961	Irish School of Landscape Painting Exhibition, King's Hall, Belfast
1948,'49	Leicester Galleries, London – 'Artists of Fame and Promise' (Group show)		
		1962,'63,'64	Royal Hibernian Academy, Dublin
1949	Kensington Art Gallery, London (Two-man show with Max Maccabe)	1963,'64	Paris Salon
		1965	'Abstractions to Writings by Ann Ruthven' New Gallery, Belfast
1949	Dawson Gallery, Dublin (Two-man show with Max Maccabe)		
		1967	'Contemporary Oil Paintings' Stafford Art Gallery and Museum, Wolverhampton Art Gallery, Scarborough Public Art Gallery.
1940s-2004	Ulster Academy/Royal Ulster Academy (Group shows)		
1950	'Contemporary Irish Paintings' Touring Exhibition, North America (Group show)	1968	Royal Institute of Oil Painters, Touring Exhibition, Shrewsbury Museum and Art Gallery, Scarborough Museum and Art Gallery, Wolverhampton Municipal Art Gallery
1950	Victor Waddington Galleries, Dublin		
1950	Ulster Artists Exhibition, Newcastle, Co. Down (Group show)		
1951	C.E.M.A., Belfast Art Gallery (Two-man show with Max Maccabe)	1969	Beechcroft Art Gallery, Southend (Group show)
1950-'60s	Oireachtais Exhibition (Group shows)	1969	Mansfield Museum and Art Gallery (Group show)
1950s-'60s	Bell Gallery, Belfast (Two-man and group shows)		
		1969	Harrrogate Art Gallery (Group show)
1952	Irish Exhibition of Living Art, Dublin and Belfast (Group shows, for several years)	1969	International House, Edinburgh
		1969	New Gallery, Belfast (One-man show)
1950s	Council for the Encouragement of Music and Arts (Group shows)	1970	Exhibition of Contemporary Oil Paintings, Art Gallery and Museum, Lichfield
1950s	John Magee Gallery, Belfast (Group shows)	1971	Exhibition of Oil Paintings, Museum and Art Gallery, Bootle
1950s-'80s	Watercolour Society of Ireland, Dublin (Group shows, each year)	1972	'Lakes, Lochs and Rivers' Touring exhibition to Municipal Galleries in Blackpool, Mansfield, Watford, Chorley, Bridlington and Southgate
195?	Mol's Art Gallery, Belfast (Group show, art and craft)		
1951	Contemporary Ulster Group, Belfast Art Gallery (Group show)	1973	Tom Caldwell Gallery, Belfast (Two-man show with Max Maccabe)
1953	'Six Ulster Artists', Belfast	1974	The Queen's University of Visual Arts Group, Belfast (Two-man show with Max Maccabe)
1952,'53	Open Air Exhibition, Rostrevor, Co. Down (Group shows)		
1954	C.E.M.A. Belfast (Two man show with Max)	1976	'Exhibition of Irish Art' Friends' School, Lisburn
1953,'54,'55	Grafton Gallery, Dublin (Group shows)	1977-2004	Ulster Watercolour Society, each year
1955	Gordon Gallery, Londonderry (Two-man show with Max)	1979,'80	Royal Hibernian Academy, Dublin
		1982,'83	Royal Hibernian Academy, Dublin
1957	John Hewitt's Private Art Collection, Belfast Art Gallery (Group show)	1984	Compton Gallery, Windsor (Group show)
		1988	Queen's University, Common Room, Belfast (Group show)
1957	Bangor Arts Club (Group show)		
1957	'Eleven Ulster Artists', Ideal Home Exhibition, Belfast	1989	James Gallery, Dalkey (Group shows)
		1989	Gladys Maccabe 'A Lifetime of Art – The Retrospective' George Gallery, Dublin
1957-'60s	The Shambles, Hillsborough, Co.Down (Open-air shows)		
		1990	'The Irish Figurists and Figurative Painting in Irish Art' George Gallery, Dublin
1958	'Seven Irish Artists' Belfast		
1958	The Art Shop, Londonderry (Two-man show with Max Maccabe)	1995	Bruton Street Gallery, London (One-man show)
1958	Toc H Room, Holywood, Co.Down (Two-man show with Max Maccabe)	1997	Stables Gallery, Ballymoney (Group show)
		1990s-2004	Eakin Gallery, Belfast (Group shows)
1958	Co-Operative Art Society, Belfast (Group show)	1990s-2004	Taylor Gallery, Belfast (Group shows)
		1990s-2004	Leinster Gallery, Dublin (Group shows)
1958	Cushendun Painting Course Exhibition, Robinson & Cleaver's, Belfast	1990s-2004	Sandford Gallery, Dublin (Group shows)
1958	Royal West of England Academy, Bristol (Group show)	1990s-2004	Bin Ban Gallery, Kerry (Group shows)
		2004	Gormley's Fine Art, Omagh and Belfast (Group Shows)
1958	Arts Council of Scotland (Two-man show with Max Maccabe)	2004	Laneside Gallery, Coleraine (Group Show)